D1225194

CAST IRON SKILLET
Dump Cakes

CAST IRON SKILLET
Dump Cakes

75 Sweet & Scrumptious Easy-to-Make Recipes

Dominique DeVito

STERLING EPICURE
New York

STERLING EPICURE
New York

An Imprint of Sterling Publishing Co., Inc.
1166 Avenue of the Americas
New York, NY 10036

STERLING EPICURE and the distinctive Sterling Epicure logo are registered trademarks of Sterling Publishing Co., Inc.

Interior text © 2018 Dominique DeVito
Cover © 2018 Sterling Publishing Co., Inc.

All rights reserved. No part of this publication may be reproduced,
stored in a retrieval system, or transmitted in any form or by any means
(including electronic, mechanical, photocopying, recording, or otherwise)
without prior written permission from the publisher.

ISBN 978-1-4549-2718-1

Distributed in Canada by Sterling Publishing Co., Inc.
c/o Canadian Manda Group, 664 Annette Street
Toronto, Ontario, M6S 2C8, Canada
Distributed in the United Kingdom by GMC Distribution Services
Castle Place, 166 High Street, Lewes, East Sussex, BN7 1XU, England
Distributed in Australia by NewSouth Books
45 Beach Street, Coogee, NSW 2034, Australia

For information about custom editions, special sales, and premium and corporate purchases,
please contact Sterling Special Sales at 800-805-5489 or specialsales@sterlingpublishing.com.

Manufactured in China

2 4 6 8 10 9 7 5 3 1

sterlingpublishing.com

Interior design by Mike Rivilis
Cover design by Elizabeth Mihaltse Lindy

Principle photography by Bill Milne/© Sterling Publishing; Additional photographs by
iStock: © Olha_Afanasieva: 145; © BWFolsom: 47 (white chocolate); © Evgeny Karandaev: 16 (lemons);
© mkos83: 89 (carrots)
Shutterstock: Africa Studio: 57; Atwood: 99 (apples); Tatiana Bralnina: 13; Natalia Bulatova: 42; Chiociolla:
63 (chocolate); Duplass: 99; Viktar Malyshchyts: 47 (rasberries); Mega Pixel: 83 (candy); Sea Wave: 18;
Tomophafan: 71; Elena Veselova: 14; Teri Virbickis: 34; Ray Yeardley: 16 (coconut)
Stocksy United: © Jeff Wasserman: 83 (ice cream)

For my brother, Robin,

whose sweet ways with all kinds of flavors

(and people) inspire me every day,

and for Dylan,

who loves a good cast iron skillet.

Contents

Introduction

Welcome to the wonderful world of cast iron skillet dump cakes—delicious desserts that are so easy to put together, you'll wonder why you ever bothered to take the time to make a fussy layer cake from scratch. Here, all you need to do is dump a cake mix and a handful of ingredients into a bowl, give them a stir, then pour the batter into a 12- or 12½-inch cast iron skillet for baking. Some forty minutes later, a big, delicious cake comes out of the oven ready to go. No layers, no frosting, and nothing more to add other than maybe a scoop of ice cream or a dab of whipped cream. I make these simple cakes all the time—whenever I want a quick snack, something for the kids after school, a last-minute dessert, or even something to serve at a dinner party or bring with me when I'm a guest.

Although savory "dump" recipes have been around for several years now, dump cakes are a recent phenomenon. Who knew that elevating a box cake mix into a fabulous cake could be so easy?

The mix allows you to skip the time-consuming task of measuring out the flour and leavening agents. But that's just the beginning. What you add beyond the eggs, oil, and water (or their substitutions) can be as creative as you like. My goal was to keep the concept of the dump cake as simple as possible while elevating its flavor and character with a few delicious additions.

But what really makes these dump cakes unique is the large 12- or 12½-inch cast iron skillet that's used as the baking vessel of choice. There are so many reasons for a cook to love a cast iron skillet, and for this collection of recipes I was reminded of the most elemental: versatility and ease. The simple skillet takes you from preparation to baking to presentation—all with delicious results. And a lot less cleanup! The virtues of this culinary tool are well known in savory cooking, but few realize how ideal the skillet can be for baking cakes. Most of these recipes start out by melting a few tablespoons of butter in the skillet to create a lovely, light-brown crust when the finished cake is flipped out of the pan. Sometimes fruit

or chocolate or coconut is added to the butter for a more exotic topping.

This book is divided into six cake flavors based on the basic cake mixes used in each category—vanilla, chocolate, carrot, spice, lemon, and strawberry. And now the fun begins. Imagine what a few pieces of Andes™ Thin Mints can do to transform a simple chocolate cake mix batter! What about cocoa powder and Rich Chocolate Ovaltine®, or peanut butter chips and peanut butter? To a basic lemon cake mix batter, perhaps add a swirl of cherry jam? Or a bit of light brown sugar and coconut flakes for a yummy topping? I let my imagination take these cakes to the next level with flavor pairings that really work. My hope is that you'll try many of these cakes, then create dump cakes of your own.

In the following sections, I'll give you more ideas for stocking your pantry, so you'll be ready to make these dump cakes whenever the urge hits you. Honestly, many of the ingredients you can add to your cakes are those you'll want to snack on anyway—unsweetened applesauce, unsweetened coconut flakes, nuts, fruits, berries, and even mini marshmallows and candies. Then I'll give you a few simple instructions so that you can keep your skillet in top shape. Turn the page, and let's get started!

preparation & adaptations

The premise of this cookbook is to show you how to make delicious cakes as simply as possible. Before I discovered the beauty of creating dump cakes in my cast iron skillet, making any cake—from scratch, or even from a box mix—involved multiple pots, pans, and cooking instruments. There were the mixing bowl(s), the measuring spoons and cups, the whisks or beaters, the cake pans and their preparation (so the batter didn't stick)—and this was just for the cake itself, never mind the frosting. It wasn't difficult, per se, but it was time-consuming at all stages, including cleanup. Of course, the results were delicious and impressive—there's no doubt about that—but I always had to think twice before taking on a cake because it was a project.

But what if you could reap the reward of a truly yummy cake without so many pots and pans to clean up, without so many measurements of this and that, and without needing to make sure the baking dish was prepared just so? It is possible, thanks to a few simple tweaks.

Simplify with a Cake Mix

First, you have to make your peace with using cake mix from a box. I know, I know. . . . It's junk, right? Not "real food." A glance at the ingredients panel isn't exactly reassuring either, but consider this: You're not eating box-mix dump cakes all day, every day; you're adding "real" ingredients like eggs, butter, and other goodies; and you're preparing something tasty and largely homemade with better quality ingredients than you'd get from a pre-packaged, grocery store cake.

Box mixes come in many different flavors, with more and more being introduced—chocolate, vanilla, white, spice, lemon, fudge, carrot, strawberry, and devil's food, to name a few. Basically, each mix contains the flour, sugar, leavening, and flavor ingredients that you otherwise would have to carefully measure out (and clean up after). And each mix requires that you add water, oil, and eggs for moisture and substance. So,

essentially, box mixes are nothing more than a base—a base to which you can add almost anything. However, all cake mixes are not created equal, even though all are supposed to yield a moist, flavorful cake. Some need three eggs, some just two. Some call for one-third cup of oil, some for half a cup. Some cake mixes even come with add-in flavor packets.

It was a revelation to me that I didn't need to strictly follow the suggested cake mix additions. While it's critical to add moisture for obvious reasons, you don't have to stick with water, vegetable oil, and eggs (though you certainly can still do this). In this cookbook, I use a variety of the most basic mixes and change up the moisture ingredients before adding my own special ingredients. As you will see, all of these simple changes make a big difference and drastically improve the flavor.

Here are some simple (and often healthier) substitutions for the basic add-ins:

Instead of water, use fruit juice, coconut water, soda, or wine.

Instead of vegetable oil, use melted butter, yogurt, sour cream, or unsweetened applesauce. (I was delighted to find that 6-ounce "large" cups

of unsweetened applesauce, the perfect amount to substitute for oil, are now available, eliminating any measuring and cleanup!)

Instead of eggs, use banana, unsweetened applesauce, silken tofu, or even peanut butter.

You can use mayonnaise as a substitute for the oil and eggs asked for in the mix. Use the same amount of mayonnaise as the recipe calls for oil, and use no eggs at all.

Embrace the Cast Iron Skillet

By using a cast iron skillet instead of baking pans, you can eliminate all the fussy pan prep work. No more spraying nonstick cooking spray on to every surface of a cake pan or greasing your cake pans with butter and then adding flour and tapping it around to cover the butter so that the batter won't stick to the side of the pan. Once the cast iron skillet is properly seasoned,

a small amount of butter or oil is all that's needed to keep foods from sticking to the surface. The more a cast iron skillet is used, the better the seasoning gets.

And with the cast iron skillet, there is no need to measure out the batter as equally as possible between two pans. In fact, there is no more worrying about layers at all. A cast iron skillet that's 12 or 12½ inches in diameter holds the full amount of batter. All you have to worry about is melting some butter in the skillet, "dumping" in the batter, baking, and then (if desired) inverting the big, single-layer cake onto a platter.

As you will quickly notice by handling its hefty weight, cast iron cookery is solid and distributes heat evenly. As a healthy bonus, a very small amount of iron is leached from the skillet into the cake but does not alter flavor. (See page 18 for more information on seasoning and caring for your cast iron skillet.)

Forget About Frosting

A classic layer cake is frosted. Frosting is typically a combination of butter, sugar, and flavoring (vanilla or chocolate, usually), and making it requires a whole other set of bowls and cooking tools. It can be messy, and it can be tricky to apply. For starters, it has to be properly allocated so you don't run out of it before you've covered the cake! While it's true that a good frosting can make or break a classic cake and a frosted layer cake is a thing of beauty as well as a great treat, making it is, well, an effort. Part of the joy of dump cakes is that you can ditch the frosting. They're fashioned so that when they're turned out of the skillet, they have good stuff on what becomes their top, so there's no need for extra sweetness. This isn't to say that the cake wouldn't be even more delicious served with whipped cream on top—and many of the recipes suggest that—but it's truly not necessary. Even the scoop of ice cream suggested to accompany many of the recipes is just a personal preference and a simple pleasure. Take it or leave it. (Okay, full disclosure here: You will find one or two frosting options in this book when I could not resist the temptation, but they are simple concoctions and just guild the lily! You can take or leave them, too.)

Dump Cake Add-Ins

Think of these add-ins as a palette and the cake mix your blank canvas, but until you're really comfortable with playing, I suggest that you follow the recipes. Some of the goodies are melted in the skillet before adding the cake batter, some are stirred into the batter itself, and some are added to the top once the batter is in the skillet. Fruit can be served along with the cakes, of course, and various spices and extracts can be added to whipped cream to serve on top of or alongside the cakes.

Fruit

Rest assured, you can use fresh, frozen, or canned fruit in a cast iron skillet dump cake, but each is going to give you a slightly different result. Fruits have various textures as well as flavors, and texture has a lot to do with how fruit holds up in a recipe. For example, the flesh of a ripe, soft-fleshed fruit, such as a peach, will be tender and succulent in a cooked cake, while the flesh of a crispy fruit, such as an apple, will remain firm and crunchy unless it's cooked for a longer amount of time. If you want to add peaches, plums, kiwis, bananas, or other soft-fleshed fruits, keep in mind that they're more fragile. Firmer-fleshed fruits, like apples, pears, or pineapple will stay true to that texture, which isn't

always what you want in a cake. I often cook them down in a bit of butter and sugar to soften before adding them to the cake batter. And, to prevent fruit from sinking to the bottom of a cake, I toss them in a bit of flour or dry cake mix before adding them to the batter.

Frozen fruits will sink when added to the batter. I dust them with flour or dry cake mix, too, and sprinkle them over the top of the cake just before I put the cake in the oven, so they'll sink more slowly.

If you want to use canned fruit, that's okay, too. They are more like compotes because they are in a liquid base already. Usually, I like to cook canned fruit down in the skillet in some butter, lemon juice, and a bit of sugar to become the bottom of the cake (or the topping when flipped out of the skillet). Canned fruit can also be stirred into the batter before being poured into the skillet.

- Apples
- Bananas
- Berries
- Cherries
- Coconut
- Lemon zest/juice
- Nectarines
- Oranges
- Peaches
- Pears
- Pineapple
- Plums
- Raisins

Spices & Extracts

Warm, nutty spices, like cinnamon, nutmeg, allspice, and clove, bring out the best in fruits and nuts, so they are used often in baking, but there are lots of other exciting options! Black and cayenne pepper, basil, and thyme are some of my favorites. Be sure to store spices in a cool, dark area to preserve their freshness.

- Allspice
- Cayenne pepper
- Cinnamon
- Cloves
- Cocoa
- Coffee

- Cumin
- Curry
- Nutmeg
- Peppermint
- Vanilla

Sweets

This category encompasses so many tasty possibilities! Baking chips are a great example. It wasn't so long ago that baking chips were semi-sweet chocolate, butterscotch, or peanut butter. Now there are dark chocolate chips, white chocolate chips, and mint chocolate chips. There are regular-size chips and mini morsels. There are even chunks. There are lots of choices, and that's just in the baking section. There are so many kinds of chocolate bars, chocolate-covered fruits, chocolate-covered hard candies, and, of course, hard candies. Again, try out a few recipes before you go out on your own.

- Candies
- Cookies
- Jams and jellies
- Maple syrup

- Chips—chocolate, white chocolate, peanut butter, and butterscotch

Dairy

Cream, sour cream, and yogurt add moisture and flavor whether in the cake or used as a type of frosting. They're also a neutral base to which other flavors can be added—everything from liqueurs and spirits to flavors like mint or coffee.

- Heavy cream
- Sour cream

- Yogurt

To Invert or Not to Invert Your Cake

The cast iron skillet makes a beautiful serving dish in which to present the cake you've baked, and it's fine to do so. However, if you keep the cake in the skillet, be sure to use a serving utensil that will not scratch the cured surface of your seasoned skillet. Hard plastic or silicon spatulas are ideal.

Also, when inverting your cake, you should know that your cake may not fall out of the skillet perfectly, the way a cake comes out of a traditional cake pan. While the surface of a well-cured skillet turns out food that doesn't stick, when you go from stovetop to oven, the likelihood of some sticking increases. All you need to do is get the hard plastic or silicon spatula gently underneath the cooked cake and gently separate it from the surface of the skillet. Sure, there's something wonderful about a cake that looks like it came from a store, but there's also something wonderful about a cake that looks like it took a wrong step along the way (so long as it's properly cooked). My mother used to say, "Pretty is as pretty does," meaning, where food is concerned, how it tastes is what's ultimately most important. Don't get caught up in how the cake looks. Touch it up with some additional fruit, a dollop of whipped cream, or ice cream. Or, when all else fails, break it into pieces and serve it with fruit and yogurt in a parfait glass. Yum!

Taking care of Your Skillet

You may be familiar with cast iron skillets. They're the black, super-heavy, one-piece pans that your grandmother always used. It cooks everything evenly—over an open fire, on the stovetop, or in the oven. It's a treasure. Some home cooks let go of their cast iron skillets when lighter pans hit the market, but that was a mistake. If you have a cast iron skillet in the family, reclaim it now. It is truly an heirloom you'll want to pass down to your own children and grandchildren.

And, while cast iron skillets may be best known as a breakfast pan, ideal for all types of "fry-ups," they can be used for baking, too. All the cakes in this cookbook are made in a 12- or 12½-inch cast iron skillet, the ideal size that will contain all the batter in each of these recipes. So, for the moment, that's the only cast iron pan you will need. But once you see how fabulous cast iron cooking can be, you'll want other sizes, too.

Cast iron does indeed last a lifetime or more, as long as it's properly cared for. It's time-consuming to season your skillet for the first time, but after that, it's just a matter of cleaning and storing it properly. Following are instructions for both seasoning your skillet before use and everyday care.

Seasoning a New or "Preseasoned" Cast Iron Skillet

Unfortunately, I did not inherit a cast iron skillet, so I needed to go shopping for a new one. I purchased a "preseasoned" Lodge pan. Lodge has been making cast iron skillets since the late 1800s, and they brand themselves as "America's Original Cookware." Recently, they developed a method to season their cookware so that it will last forever, as it always has, but with minimal consistent care. They coat the pan with vegetable oil and bake the oil into the pan at a very

high heat—just what you need to do to an unseasoned pan. While the idea is that you can start cooking in a "preseasoned" cast iron skillet immediately—and you can—it's still a good idea to go through the process of establishing a seasoned finish to the pan before you cook with it. Here's how:

1. Position the oven racks in the middle and lower thirds of the oven and preheat the oven to 450°F.

2. Put ½ cup kosher salt in the skillet. Rub it all over the bottom and sides to remove any impurities.

3. Wash the skillet with dish soap and hot water (you will not be using soapy water to wash it once it's seasoned), and thoroughly dry the skillet with a cloth or paper towels.

4. Soak a bit of paper towel in an unsaturated fat—vegetable or canola oil is best—and rub the oil all over the skillet. (Don't use olive oil; it's a saturated fat and isn't as reactive to the surface of the skillet.)

5. Put the skillet on the middle rack of the preheated oven, upside down, with a piece of foil or a cookie sheet on the bottom rack to catch any drips, and leave it in the oven for 30 minutes. (The pan may smoke, and its surface will become very dark.)

6. Remove the skillet from the oven, and let it cool.

7. Repeat this procedure three or four times until the skillet is nearly pitch-black, then turn off the oven and let the skillet cool completely.

Everyday Care

The more you use the skillet, the more resistant the surface will be to food sticking. The trick is to clean the pan immediately after using it, while it is still hot and without using soap. First, allow it to cool just a bit to the point where you can work with it. Using a moderately abrasive sponge, like a Dobie™, or a special cast iron cleaning sponge or brush, lightly press against the surface to remove any stuck-on food. Rinse under warm water as you do so.

When the surface is free of food particles, put the wet pan back on the stove. Turn on the burner, allow the skillet to dry, then remove from the heat. Holding the handle with a pot holder, put some vegetable or canola oil in the pan and rub it all over with a paper towel. Allow the skillet to cool to room temperature, then use another paper towel to wipe away any residual oil on the surface, though there shouldn't be any.

The trick is to clean your cast iron skillet immediately after use. Removing food debris from a hot pan is much easier than from one that has been allowed to cool, and you will be able to avoid scrubbing off the seasoning, too. Avoid tough abrasives. These include metal scrubby scouring pads. And remember: No soap or cleaners of any kind.

Remember:

RULE #1: *Never wash your seasoned pan with soapy water!*

RULE #2: *Never put a cast iron pan in the dishwasher!*

Why? This breaks down the protective seasoning, and you'll have to reseason the pan all over again. Leaving any kind of water on the pan will lead to rusting, which will also require reseasoning. Store your skillet where there is good air circulation so moisture doesn't get trapped on the surface. If you need to stack it, put paper towels on the top and bottom.

Vanilla Cakes

THE WORD *VANILLA* is often used to imply that something is ordinary, but I assure you, these cakes are anything but ho-hum. I simply chose the word *vanilla* as an umbrella for all the plain box cake mixes that serve as the foundation for these cakes. In fact, the mixes are labeled everything from Vanilla and French Vanilla to Golden, Butter, and Yellow. With each, you are starting with a neutral base, so you can add almost anything and take your dump cake in any direction you'd like. As you will see, I experimented with everything from fruit and nuts, to marshmallows and candy, to rum and coconut, to chocolate chips and caramel, to coffee and half-and-half, to orange juice and soda. I even created a spicy cake flavored with pepitas and cayenne! There are twenty recipes in this chapter, but I bet you can come up with a dozen more to satisfy your own flavor preferences and those of your family. All kinds of crushed cookies or dried fruits come to mind. The idea is to keep it simple and flavorful.

Coconut-Brown Sugar Cake

It's so great to make cakes that don't need frosting! Here, a brown sugar and butter mixture that coats the batter as it cooks adds all the extra deliciousness that a frosting would, and it's infinitely easier.

TIME: 1 hour

SERVES 8

4 tablespoons butter

2 tablespoons dark brown sugar

1 box white cake mix

1 cup unsweetened coconut flakes

½ cup unsweetened shredded coconut

1¼ cups water

⅓ cup vegetable oil

6 ounces unsweetened applesauce

3 large eggs

Vanilla ice cream and raspberry or chocolate sauce, for serving (optional)

Preheat the oven to 350°F.

Melt the butter in a 12- or 12½-inch cast iron skillet over low heat, then sprinkle the brown sugar over the butter and let the sugar melt. Keep warm over low heat while preparing the batter. Don't let the butter burn. If your burner has a very low setting, that's best. If the mixture starts to brown, remove the skillet from the burner.

Combine the cake mix, coconut flakes, shredded coconut, water, oil, applesauce, and eggs in a large bowl and stir until well combined.

Pour the batter over the brown sugar mixture in the skillet. (The sugar mixture will come up over the sides of the batter. It's all part of the magic.)

Bake the cake for 30 to 40 minutes, or until browned on the top and sides and a toothpick inserted in the center comes out clean.

Remove the cake from the oven and let it cool in the skillet for 10 minutes. The skillet will still be hot. Cover a baking sheet with foil and invert it on top of the skillet. Wearing oven mitts, hold the edge of the sheet and the large handle of the skillet with one hand and use the other hand as a guide to keep the sheet and skillet together as you turn them over as a unit. Remove the skillet from the inverted cake, then use an offset spatula to slide the cake from the sheet to a large plate.

Let the cake cool, then serve with vanilla ice cream and a drizzle of raspberry or chocolate sauce.

Fruit Cup Cake

This cake defines the simplicity of a "dump" cake, where you just throw in some colorful fruit and chocolate morsels, if desired, to liven up a basic cake mix. The fruit cup is baked into the cake, like an upside-down cake, and plenty of butter and applesauce make it super moist. Your kids will love this one, and you will, too.

TIME: 1 hour

SERVES 8

½ cup (1 stick) butter

1 (15-ounce) can mixed fruit (no sugar added), drained

1 box yellow cake mix

1 cup water

½ cup vegetable oil

6 ounces unsweetened applesauce

3 large eggs

1 cup mini semi-sweet chocolate morsels (optional)

Preheat the oven to 350°F.

Melt the butter in a 12- or 12½-inch cast iron skillet over medium heat. Add the mixed fruit, distributing evenly, then reduce the heat to low and continue to warm the fruit while preparing the batter.

Combine the cake mix, water, oil, applesauce, and eggs in a large bowl and stir to combine.

When the fruit mixture in the skillet just starts to bubble, pour the batter over it.

Bake the cake for 35 to 40 minutes, or until golden brown and a toothpick inserted in the center comes out clean.

Remove the cake from the oven and let it cool in the skillet for 10 minutes. The skillet will still be hot. Cover a baking sheet with foil and invert it on top of the skillet. Wearing oven mitts, hold the edge of the sheet and the large handle of the skillet with one hand and use the other hand as a guide to keep the sheet and skillet together as you turn them over as a unit. Remove the skillet from the inverted cake, then use an offset spatula to slide the cake from the sheet to a large plate.

Let the cake cool to room temperature before serving.

Orange Creamsicle Cake

I was delighted to come across recipes for dump cakes that involved nothing more than a boxed mix and a can of soda. Wow! I had to try it. While it's true that you can make such a cake, I couldn't resist jazzing it up a bit.

TIME: 45 minutes

SERVES 8

2 tablespoons butter

¼ cup orange juice (preferably with pulp)

1 tablespoon light brown sugar (optional)

1 box yellow cake mix

1 (20-ounce) can orange soda (diet is okay)

Toasted whole almonds, for garnish

Fruit-flavored frozen yogurt or fine-quality vanilla ice cream, for serving

Preheat the oven to 350°F.

Melt the butter in a 12- or 12½-inch cast iron skillet over low heat, then add the orange juice and swirl the skillet to combine. Sprinkle the brown sugar over the mixture and keep warm on very low heat while preparing the batter. Don't let the mixture burn. If your burner has a very low setting, that's best. If the mixture gets too brown, remove the skillet from the burner.

Combine the cake mix and soda in a large bowl and stir until smooth.

Pour the batter over the orange juice mixture in the skillet.

Bake the cake for 35 to 40 minutes, or until a toothpick inserted in the center comes out clean.

Remove the cake from the oven and let it cool in the skillet for 10 minutes. The skillet will still be hot. Cover a baking sheet with foil and invert it on top of the skillet. Wearing oven mitts, hold the edge of the sheet and the large handle of the skillet with one hand and use the other hand as a guide to keep the sheet and skillet together as you turn them over as a unit. Remove the skillet from the inverted cake, then use an offset spatula to slide the cake from the sheet to a large plate.

Let the cake cool, then sprinkle with a few toasted almonds and serve with frozen yogurt or vanilla ice cream.

Goofy Grape Cake

Okay, this cake is funky. I'm still not sure how I feel about it, but I can tell you this: Kids love it. The grape "glaze" adds additional color and flavor. For a fruity treat, serve with strawberry ice cream.

TIME: 45 minutes

SERVES 8

2 tablespoons butter

¼ cup grape jam or jelly

1 box white cake mix

1 (20-ounce) can grape soda (diet is okay)

Strawberry ice cream, for serving (optional)

Preheat the oven to 350°F.

Melt the butter in a 12- or 12½-inch cast iron skillet over low heat, then add the jam or jelly and stir until combined. Keep warm over low heat while preparing the batter. If your burner has a very low setting, that's best. If the mixture starts to brown, remove the skillet from the burner.

Combine the cake mix with the soda in a large bowl and stir until smooth.

Pour the batter over the jelly mixture in the skillet.

Bake the cake for 35 to 40 minutes, or until a toothpick inserted in the center comes out clean.

Remove the cake from the oven and let it cool in the skillet for 10 minutes. The skillet will still be hot. Cover a baking sheet with foil and invert it on top of the skillet. Wearing oven mitts, hold the edge of the sheet and the large handle of the skillet with one hand and use the other hand as a guide to keep the sheet and skillet together as you turn them over as a unit. Remove the skillet from the inverted cake, then use an offset spatula to slide the cake from the sheet to a large plate.

Let the cake cool, then serve with strawberry ice cream.

pumpkin-cream cheesecake

If you want a moist cake that's not too sweet, this one's for you. Puréed pumpkin has lots of fiber and no sugar. Balance it with a hint of maple syrup and some additional butter, and you have a cake that is sweet enough for dessert (especially with whipped cream, ice cream, or a caramel sauce on top) but savory enough to have as a snack with a cup of coffee or tea.

TIME: 1 hour

SERVES 8

2 tablespoons butter

1 box vanilla cake mix

1 cup (8 ounces) pumpkin purée

2 large eggs

½ cup water

4 ounces cream cheese, cut into small cubes

2 tablespoons plus ¼ cup 100% natural maple syrup (preferably Grade B)

Whipped cream, ice cream, or caramel sauce, for serving (optional)

Preheat the oven to 350°F.

Melt the butter in a 12- or 12½-inch cast iron skillet over low heat while preparing the batter. Don't let the butter burn. If your burner has a very low setting, that's best. If the butter starts to brown, remove the skillet from the burner.

Combine the cake mix, pumpkin purée, eggs, and water in a large bowl and beat with an electric mixer or stir just until smooth. Beat or stir in the cream cheese.

Drizzle 2 tablespoons of the maple syrup over the melted butter in the skillet, then pour the batter over the top. Drizzle the remaining ¼ cup maple syrup over the top of the batter.

Bake the cake for 35 to 40 minutes, or until a toothpick inserted in the center comes out clean.

Remove the cake from the oven and let it cool in the skillet for 10 minutes. The skillet will still be hot. Cover a baking sheet with foil and invert it on top of the skillet. Wearing oven mitts, hold the edge of the sheet and the large handle of the skillet with one hand and use the other hand as a guide to keep the sheet and skillet together as you turn them over as a unit. Remove the skillet from the inverted cake, then use an offset spatula to slide the cake from the sheet to a large plate.

Let the cake cool, then serve with whipped cream, ice cream, or caramel sauce.

Variation: *Why not guild the lily and frost this cake with my favorite cream cheese frosting (see photo)! First, let* **8 ounces cream cheese** *soften. Cut* **½ cup (1 stick) butter** *into little pieces and let that soften, too. Then, blend the cream cheese in a large bowl with an electric mixer on low speed until smooth. Add the pieces of butter, one by one, beating on low or medium speed until each piece is incorporated. Add* **1 cup confectioners' sugar** *and beat on medium speed until just combined. Finally, add* **1 teaspoon vanilla extract** *and continue to beat until the frosting is well blended and creamy. Once the cake is cool, frost and refrigerate. When ready to serve, drizzle with* **caramel sauce** *and sprinkle with a few* **chopped walnuts**.

peach-pecan cake

This sensational cake combines the flavors of the south— pecans, peaches, butter, and a splash of bourbon. At the height of peach season, when peaches are very ripe and plentiful, you'll want to use fresh fruit. (Make sure your peaches are very ripe, then peel and slice them, or cut them into bits. You'll also need to replace the canned juice in the batter mixture with 1 cup water and ½ cup vegetable oil.)

TIME: 1 hour

SERVES 8

2 tablespoons butter

2 tablespoons dark brown sugar

1 tablespoon bourbon (optional)

1 (20-ounce) can sliced peaches (juices reserved)

1 box golden butter cake mix

2 large eggs

1 teaspoon vanilla extract

¼ teaspoon nutmeg

½ cup crushed (pea-size) pecan pieces

Crème fraîche, Greek yogurt, or fresh whipped cream, for serving

Preheat the oven to 350°F.

Melt the butter in a 12- or 12½-inch cast iron skillet over low heat. Add the brown sugar and bourbon, if using, and stir gently until combined and the sugar is melted. Scatter the peach slices over the mixture and keep warm while preparing the batter.

Combine the peach juice, cake mix, eggs, vanilla extract, and nutmeg in a large bowl and beat with an electric mixer or stir until smooth. Stir in the pecan pieces.

Pour the batter over the peach mixture in the skillet.

Bake the cake for 35 to 40 minutes, or until a toothpick inserted in the center comes out clean.

Remove the cake from the oven and let it cool in the skillet for 10 minutes. The skillet will still be hot. Cover a baking sheet with foil and invert it on top of the skillet. Wearing oven mitts, hold the edge of the sheet and the large handle of the skillet with one hand and use the other hand as a guide to keep the sheet and skillet together as you turn them over as a unit. Remove the skillet from the inverted cake, then use an offset spatula to slide the cake from the sheet to a large plate.

Let the cake cool, then serve with crème fraîche, Greek yogurt, or fresh whipped cream.

pumpkin-pecan cake

I'm a sucker for pumpkin. First of all, I love the flavor, but I also love that it has lots of fiber and beta-carotene, too. Add a brown sugar–pecan crust for a fabulous treat.

TIME: 1 hour

SERVES 8

3 tablespoons butter

¼ cup 100% natural maple syrup (preferably Grade B)

½ cup pecan pieces, broken into smaller bits

1 box vanilla cake mix

1 cup (8 ounces) pumpkin purée

2 large eggs

½ cup water

¼ teaspoon vanilla extract

Whipped cream or vanilla ice cream, for serving (optional)

Preheat the oven to 350°F.

Melt the butter in a 12- or 12½-inch cast iron skillet over low heat. Stir together the maple syrup and pecan pieces in a small bowl, then add the melted butter and stir until combined. Don't wipe out the butter that remains in the skillet. Set aside.

Combine the cake mix, pumpkin purée, eggs, water, and vanilla extract in a large bowl and beat with an electric mixer or stir until smooth.

Pour the batter into the skillet. Working with your fingers, evenly distribute the pecan mixture over the batter.

Bake the cake for 35 to 40 minutes, or until a toothpick inserted in the center comes out clean.

Remove the cake from the oven and let it cool in the skillet for 10 minutes. The skillet will still be hot. Cover a baking sheet with foil and invert it on top of the skillet. Wearing oven mitts, hold the edge of the sheet and the large handle of the skillet with one hand and use the other hand as a guide to keep the sheet and skillet together as you turn them over as a unit. Remove the skillet from the inverted cake, then use an offset spatula to slide the cake from the sheet to a large plate.

Let the cake cool, then serve with whipped cream or vanilla ice cream.

Blueberry almond cake

Using frozen fruit instead of canned makes for a lighter cake, but you can also use fresh berries if you have them. Sprinkling the berries on top of the batter just before baking the cake prevents them from sinking to the bottom.

TIME: 1 hour

SERVES 8

3 tablespoons butter

1 box yellow cake mix

2 large eggs

½ cup vegetable oil

6 ounces unsweetened applesauce

½ teaspoon almond extract

1 (12-ounce) bag frozen blueberries

¼ cup dark brown sugar

Whipped cream, for serving (optional)

Preheat the oven to 350°F.

Melt the butter in a 12- or 12½-inch cast iron skillet over low heat while preparing the batter. Don't let the butter burn. If your burner has a very low setting, that's best. If the butter starts to brown, remove the skillet from the burner.

Combine the cake mix, eggs, oil, applesauce, and almond extract in a large bowl and beat with an electric mixer or stir until smooth.

Pour the batter over the butter in the skillet. Sprinkle the blueberries and brown sugar evenly over the top.

Bake the cake for 35 to 40 minutes, or until a toothpick inserted in the center comes out clean.

Remove the cake from the oven and let it cool in the skillet for 10 minutes. The skillet will still be hot. Cover a baking sheet with foil and invert it on top of the skillet. Wearing oven mitts, hold the edge of the sheet and the large handle of the skillet with one hand and use the other hand as a guide to keep the sheet and skillet together as you turn them over as a unit. Remove the skillet from the inverted cake, then use an offset spatula to slide the cake from the sheet to a large plate.

Let the cake cool, then serve with whipped cream.

cherry almond cake

You might not expect all the flavor combinations in this little cake to produce such a wonderful result, but they do. Almond extract has a way of both tempering and enhancing the sweetness of the cherries, and a tad of Amaretto liqueur brings it all home.

TIME: 1 hour

SERVES 8

2 tablespoons butter

1 tablespoon Amaretto liqueur

1½ cups pitted cherries, whole or halved, or
    1 (20-ounce) can cherries, drained

1 box yellow cake mix

2 large eggs

6 ounces unsweetened applesauce

½ teaspoon almond extract

Confectioners' sugar, for garnish (optional)

Whipped cream or ice cream, for serving (optional)

Preheat the oven to 350°F.

Melt the butter in a 12- or 12½-inch cast iron skillet over low heat, then add the Amaretto liqueur and swirl the skillet to combine. Keep warm over low heat while preparing the batter. Don't let the mixture burn. If your burner has a very low setting, that's best. If the mixture starts to bubble, remove the skillet from the burner.

If using fresh cherries, put them in a small bowl and sprinkle with some of the cake mix.

Combine the remaining cake mix, eggs, applesauce, and almond extract in a large bowl and beat with an electric mixer or stir until smooth. Stir in the cherries.

Pour the batter over the Amaretto mixture in the skillet.

Bake the cake for 30 to 40 minutes, or until a toothpick inserted in the center comes out clean.

Remove the cake from the oven and let it cool in the skillet for 10 minutes. The skillet will still be hot. Cover a baking sheet with foil and invert it on top of the skillet. Wearing oven mitts, hold the edge of the sheet and the large handle of the skillet with one hand and use the other hand as a guide to keep the sheet and skillet together as you turn them over as a unit. Remove the skillet from the inverted cake, then use an offset spatula to slide the cake from the sheet to a large plate.

Let the cake cool, then dust with confectioners' sugar, if desired, and serve with whipped cream or ice cream.

apple-cranberry-walnut cake

This is a fall favorite in my house, and who can resist? This cake has all kinds of goodies inside, but the apples are the star of the show. In this recipe, I prefer varieties that are really crisp and crunchy, like Granny Smith or Gala.

TIME: 1½ hours

SERVES 8

2 tablespoons butter

1 box golden butter cake mix

3 large eggs

½ cup vegetable oil

6 ounces unsweetened applesauce

¼ teaspoon ground cinnamon

¼ teaspoon ground nutmeg

2 medium apples, peeled, seeded, and cut into small cubes

¼ cup dried cranberries

¼ cup walnut pieces, chopped

Preheat the oven to 350°F.

Melt the butter in a 12- or 12½-inch cast iron skillet over low heat while preparing the batter. Don't let the butter burn. If your burner has a very low setting, that's best. If the butter starts to brown, remove the skillet from the burner.

Combine the cake mix, eggs, oil, applesauce, cinnamon, and nutmeg in a large bowl and stir until smooth.

Pour the batter over the butter in the skillet. Combine the apples, cranberries, and walnut pieces in a small bowl and distribute evenly over the batter.

Bake the cake for 35 to 40 minutes, or until a toothpick inserted in the center comes out clean.

Remove the cake from the oven and let it cool in the skillet for 10 minutes. The skillet will still be hot. Cover a baking sheet with foil and invert it on top of the skillet. Wearing oven mitts, hold the edge of the sheet and the large handle of the skillet with one hand and use the other hand as a guide to keep the sheet and skillet together as you turn them over as a unit. Remove the skillet from the inverted cake, then use an offset spatula to slide the cake from the sheet to a large plate.

Let the cake cool before serving.

sweet and spicy cake

If you like the combination of sweet and spicy flavors, you should give this cake a spin. The addition of yogurt tones down the sweetness to better complement the spicy pumpkin seed and cayenne topping. As an added surprise, you really should try a still-warm slice with an ice-cold beer. No, I'm not kidding!

TIME: 1 hour

SERVES 8

4 tablespoons butter

½ cup spiced pepitas (green pumpkin seeds)

¼ teaspoon cayenne pepper

1 tablespoon light brown sugar

1 box yellow cake mix

3 large eggs

1 cup plain yogurt

Cold beer or sparkling cider, for serving (optional)

Preheat the oven to 350°F.

Melt the butter in a 12- or 12½-inch cast iron skillet over low heat, then stir in the pepitas, cayenne pepper, and brown sugar. Keep warm over low heat while preparing the batter. Don't let the mixture burn. If your burner has a very low setting, that's best. If the mixture starts to brown, remove the skillet from the burner.

Combine the cake mix, eggs, and yogurt in a large bowl and stir until smooth.

Pour the batter over the pepita mixture in the skillet.

Bake the cake for 30 to 40 minutes, or until a toothpick inserted in the center comes out clean.

Remove the cake from the oven and let it cool in the skillet for 10 minutes. The skillet will still be hot. Cover a baking sheet with foil and invert it on top of the skillet. Wearing oven mitts, hold the edge of the sheet and the large handle of the skillet with one hand and use the other hand as a guide to keep the sheet and skillet together as you turn them over as a unit. Remove the skillet from the inverted cake, then use an offset spatula to slide the cake from the sheet to a large plate.

Serve the cake immediately, ideally with a nice cold beer or sparkling cider.

Mixed Berry Cake with almonds

Although this cake is made with frozen berries (they hold up better in the batter), I like to make it during the summertime when I can serve it right in the skillet along with fresh berries and whipped cream, of course. It's easy to make, and you don't need to keep the oven on for very long.

TIME: 1 hour

SERVES 8

1 (12- or 16-ounce) bag frozen mixed berries

2 tablespoons butter

½ cup sliced almonds

1 box white cake mix

3 large eggs

6 ounces unsweetened applesauce

⅓ cup vegetable oil

½ teaspoon almond extract

Fresh mixed fruit, for serving (optional)

Confectioners' sugar, for garnish (optional)

Preheat the oven to 350°F.

Put the frozen berries in a microwave-safe bowl and microwave on high for 2 minutes. (Or, if you have time, you can just thaw them in a bowl.) Set aside.

Melt the butter in a 12- or 12½-inch cast iron skillet over low heat. Arrange the sliced almonds in the butter and keep warm over low heat while preparing the batter. Don't let the mixture burn. If your burner has a very low setting, that's best. If the butter or nuts start to brown, remove the skillet from the burner.

Combine the cake mix, eggs, applesauce, oil, and almond extract in a large bowl and beat with an electric mixer or stir until smooth. Add the thawed berries and any juice accumulated in the bowl and stir until well combined.

Pour the batter over the almonds and butter in the skillet.

Bake the cake for 35 to 40 minutes, or until a toothpick inserted in the center comes out clean.

Remove the cake from the oven and let it cool in the skillet for 10 minutes. The skillet will still be hot. Cover a baking sheet with foil and invert it on top of the skillet. Wearing oven mitts, hold the edge of the sheet and the large handle of the skillet with one hand and use the other hand as a guide to keep the sheet and skillet together as you turn them over as a unit. Remove the skillet from the inverted cake, then use an offset spatula to slide the cake from the sheet to a large plate.

Let the cake cool, then serve, topped with fresh fruit and a dusting of confectioners' sugar.

strawberry-Rhubarb cake

Rhubarb, a perennial plant rich in fiber and vitamin K, is actually a vegetable, though the stalks are most often cooked with sugar to tame their tartness (the leaves, by the way, are poisonous). The plant requires the cold of winter to grow, and since it is harvested in late spring/ early summer, strawberries are the natural pairing. The classic combo brings this cake to life.

TIME: 1 hour

SERVES 8

1 cup fresh rhubarb slices (¼-inch thick)

1 cup strawberries, quartered

1 tablespoon light brown sugar

2 tablespoons butter

1 box golden butter cake mix

3 large eggs

6 ounces unsweetened applesauce

⅓ cup vegetable oil

Whipped cream or Greek yogurt, for serving (optional)

Preheat the oven to 350°F.

Combine the rhubarb and strawberry pieces with the brown sugar in a bowl and stir to combine well.

Melt the butter in a 12- or 12½-inch cast iron skillet over low heat while preparing the batter. Don't let the butter burn. If your burner has a very low setting, that's best. If the butter starts to brown, remove the skillet from the burner.

Combine the cake mix, eggs, applesauce, and oil in a large bowl and stir until smooth.

Pour half of the batter over the butter in the skillet, then sprinkle the strawberry-rhubarb mixture evenly over the batter. Top with the remaining batter.

Bake the cake for 40 to 45 minutes, or until a toothpick inserted in the center comes out clean.

Remove the cake from the oven and let it cool in the skillet for 10 minutes. The skillet will still be hot. Cover a baking sheet with foil and invert it on top of the skillet. Wearing oven mitts, hold the edge of the sheet and the large handle of the skillet with one hand and use the other hand as a guide to keep the sheet and skillet together as you turn them over as a unit. Remove the skillet from the inverted cake, then use an offset spatula to slide the cake from the sheet to a large plate.

Let the cake cool, then serve with whipped cream or Greek yogurt.

Cinnamon-Sour Cream Cake

Cinnamon-sour cream coffee cake with streusel topping is a beloved classic. This recipe lets you skip the preparation time and extra calories of the streusel topping but still offers full cinnamon-sour cream goodness. Ready?

TIME: 1 hour

SERVES 8

2 tablespoons butter

½ teaspoon cinnamon

1 box yellow cake mix

2 large eggs

½ cup vegetable oil

1 cup (8 ounces) sour cream

1 (10-ounce) package cinnamon chips

2 tablespoons dark brown sugar

Butter pecan ice cream, for serving (optional)

Preheat the oven to 350°F.

Melt the butter in a 12- or 12½-inch cast iron skillet over low heat, then sprinkle the cinnamon evenly over the butter. Keep warm over low heat while preparing the batter. Don't let the butter burn. If your burner has a very low setting, that's best. If the butter starts to brown, remove the skillet from the burner.

Combine the cake mix, eggs, oil, and sour cream in a large bowl and stir until smooth.

Pour the batter over the cinnamon mixture in the skillet, then sprinkle the cinnamon chips and brown sugar evenly over the top.

Bake the cake for 35 to 40 minutes, or until a toothpick inserted in the center comes out clean.

Remove the cake from the oven and let it cool in the skillet for 10 minutes. The skillet will still be hot. Cover a baking sheet with foil and invert it on top of the skillet. Wearing oven mitts, hold the edge of the sheet and the large handle of the skillet with one hand and use the other hand as a guide to keep the sheet and skillet together as you turn them over as a unit. Remove the skillet from the inverted cake, then use an offset spatula to slide the cake from the sheet to a large plate.

Let the cake cool, then serve with butter pecan ice cream.

caramel-chocolate chip cake

When I noticed a new pudding flavor—caramel—at the grocery store, I knew that I had to somehow blend it into a dump cake. I'm so glad I did.

TIME: 75 minutes

SERVES 8

2 tablespoons butter

1 (3.4-ounce) package caramel-flavored instant pudding

2 cups cold milk

1 box yellow cake mix

2 large eggs

1 cup chocolate chips

Vanilla ice cream or unsweetened whipped cream, for serving (optional)

Preheat the oven to 350°F.

Melt the butter in a 12- or 12½-inch cast iron skillet over very low heat while preparing the batter. Don't let the butter burn. If your burner has a very low setting, that's best. If the butter starts to brown, remove the skillet from the burner.

Combine the instant pudding and milk in a large bowl and whisk for about 2 minutes. Add the cake mix and eggs to the pudding and stir vigorously until smooth. Stir in the chocolate chips.

Pour the batter over the butter in the skillet.

Bake the cake for 45 to 50 minutes, or until a toothpick inserted in the center comes out clean.

Remove the cake from the oven and let it cool in the skillet for 10 minutes. The skillet will still be hot. Cover a baking sheet with foil and invert it on top of the skillet. Wearing oven mitts, hold the edge of the sheet and the large handle of the skillet with one hand and use the other hand as a guide to keep the sheet and skillet together as you turn them over as a unit. Remove the skillet from the inverted cake, then use an offset spatula to slide the cake from the sheet to a large plate.

Let the cake cool, then serve with vanilla ice cream or unsweetened whipped cream.

Raspberry-White Chocolate Cake

If you are a white chocolate fan who loves raspberries, you really should give this pretty cake a try. And, if you really want to doll it up, see the Variation, right.

TIME: 1 hour

SERVES 8

2 tablespoons butter

1 box white cake mix

2 large eggs

½ cup vegetable oil

¾ cup water

1 (12-ounce) bag frozen raspberries

1 cup white chocolate chips

Preheat the oven to 350°F.

Melt the butter in a 12- or 12½-inch cast iron skillet over low heat while preparing the batter. Don't let the butter burn. If your burner has a very low setting, that's best. If the butter starts to brown, remove the skillet from the burner.

Combine the cake mix, eggs, oil, and water in a large bowl and stir until smooth. Add the frozen raspberries and stir until well combined.

Pour the batter over the butter in the skillet and sprinkle the white chocolate chips evenly over the top.

Bake the cake for 30 to 35 minutes, or until a toothpick inserted in the center comes out clean.

Remove the cake from the oven and let it cool in the skillet for 10 minutes. The skillet will still be hot. Cover a baking sheet with foil and invert it on top of the skillet. Wearing oven mitts, hold the edge of the sheet and the large handle of the skillet with one hand and use the other hand as a guide to keep the sheet and skillet together as you turn them over as a unit. Remove the skillet from the inverted cake, then use an offset spatula to slide the cake from the sheet to a large plate.

Let the cake cool before serving.

Variation: *For a more formal presentation, slice the cake in half with a serrated knife to make two thin layers, fill the cake with bottled raspberry jam, and top the cake with buttercream frosting or fresh whipped cream. Buttercream frosting is easy to make and so much better than canned frosting. To make it from scratch: Cream together* ½ **cup (1 stick) softened unsalted butter** *and* 1½ **cups confectioners' sugar** *in a large mixing bowl with an electric mixer on low speed until blended. Add* **1 tablespoon heavy cream** *and* ½ **teaspoon vanilla extract** *and beat on high speed until just combined. Stir with a spoon to make sure the frosting is thoroughly combined, then spread on the cooled cake.*

Party Cake

Making a cake filled with colored sprinkles isn't just for kids. It's a great way to get your weekend off to a fun start, end it with a bit of a celebration, or get everyone in the family happily through the middle of the week. To provide a real party atmosphere, offer several kinds of frostings to put on the slices of cake. And more sprinkles, of course.

TIME: 1 hour

SERVES 8

2 tablespoons butter

1 box yellow or white cake mix

3 large eggs

6 ounces unsweetened applesauce

⅓ cup vegetable oil

⅓ cup water

½ teaspoon vanilla extract

2 to 3 tablespoons multi-colored sprinkles

Various frostings, for serving (optional)

Preheat the oven to 350°F.

Melt the butter in a 12- or 12½-inch cast iron skillet over low heat while preparing the batter. Don't let the butter burn. If your burner has a very low setting, that's best. If the butter starts to brown, remove the skillet from the burner.

Combine the cake mix, eggs, applesauce, oil, water, and vanilla extract and beat with an electric mixer or stir until smooth. Stir in the sprinkles.

Pour the batter over the butter in the skillet.

Bake the cake for 30 to 40 minutes, or until a toothpick inserted in the center comes out clean.

Remove the cake from the oven and let it cool in the skillet for 10 minutes. The skillet will still be hot. Cover a baking sheet with foil and invert it on top of the skillet. Wearing oven mitts, hold the edge of the sheet and the large handle of the skillet with one hand and use the other hand as a guide to keep the sheet and skillet together as you turn them over as a unit. Remove the skillet from the inverted cake, then use an offset spatula to slide the cake from the sheet to a large plate.

Let the cake cool before serving as is or with frosting of your choice.

mini marshmallow candy cake

If you want to get your kids excited about baking, have them help you with this cake. The preparation couldn't be easier, and the result is delicious. Keep this cake in mind as a great birthday party cake—no frosting required. Add a few colorful candles, and you're good to go!

TIME: 1 hour

SERVES 8 TO 10

2 tablespoons butter

1 box yellow cake mix

3 large eggs

1 cup water

½ cup vegetable oil

1 cup mini marshmallows

1 (2-ounce) bag candy decors (rainbow chips) or ¼ cup mini M&M's®

Preheat the oven to 350°F.

Melt the butter in a 12- or 12½-inch cast iron skillet over low heat while preparing the batter. Don't let the butter burn. If your burner has a very low setting, that's best. If the butter starts to brown, remove the skillet from the burner.

Combine the cake mix, eggs, water, and oil in a large bowl and stir until smooth. Add the mini marshmallows and candies and stir until well combined.

Pour the batter over the butter in the skillet.

Bake the cake for 30 to 35 minutes, or until a toothpick inserted in the center comes out clean.

Remove the cake from the oven and let it cool in the skillet for 10 minutes. The skillet will still be hot. Cover a baking sheet with foil and invert it on top of the skillet. Wearing oven mitts, hold the edge of the sheet and the large handle of the skillet with one hand and use the other hand as a guide to keep the sheet and skillet together as you turn them over as a unit. Remove the skillet from the inverted cake, then use an offset spatula to slide the cake from the sheet to a large plate.

Let the cake cool before serving.

Latte cake

If you're a fan of coffee with steamed milk, you're going to love this cake. Keep it in mind for the next time you invite a few friends over for a lazy afternoon get-together.

TIME: 1 hour

SERVES 8

2 tablespoons butter

1 teaspoon instant coffee or espresso

1 box yellow cake mix

½ cup cold coffee

½ cup half-and-half

2 large eggs

⅓ cup vegetable oil

Preheat the oven to 350°F.

Melt the butter in a 12- or 12½-inch cast iron skillet over low heat, then add the instant coffee or espresso and stir to combine. Keep warm over low heat while preparing the batter. Don't let the mixture burn. If your burner has a very low setting, that's best. If the mixture starts to bubble, remove the skillet from the burner.

Combine the cake mix, coffee, half-and-half, eggs, and oil in a large bowl and beat with an electric mixer or stir until smooth.

Pour the batter over the coffee mixture in the skillet.

Bake the cake for 30 to 40 minutes, or until a toothpick inserted in the center comes out clean.

Remove the cake from the oven and let it cool in the skillet for 10 minutes. The skillet will still be hot. Cover a baking sheet with foil and invert it on top of the skillet. Wearing oven mitts, hold the edge of the sheet and the large handle of the skillet with one hand and use the other hand as a guide to keep the sheet and skillet together as you turn them over as a unit. Remove the skillet from the inverted cake, then use an offset spatula to slide the cake from the sheet to a large plate.

Let the cake cool before serving.

Piña Colada Cake

If you love the tropical flavors of pineapple and coconut, you won't be able to resist this cake. There's even a butter-rum topping. Irresistible!

TIME: 1 hour

SERVES 8

2 tablespoons butter

2 tablespoons dark rum

1 box white cake mix

½ cup coconut milk

2 large eggs

1 cup strained crushed pineapple (plus additional for serving, optional)

½ cup unsweetened coconut flakes

Whipped cream, coconut gelato, toasted coconut, pineapple chunks, and a maraschino cherry, for serving (optional)

Preheat the oven to 350°F.

Melt the butter in a 12- or 12½-inch cast iron skillet over low heat, then stir in the rum. Keep warm over low heat while preparing the batter. If your burner has a very low setting, that's best. If the mixture starts to bubble, remove the skillet from the burner.

Combine the cake mix, coconut milk, and eggs in a large bowl and stir until smooth. Add the pineapple and coconut flakes and stir to combine well.

Pour the batter over the rum mixture in the skillet.

Bake the cake for 30 to 35 minutes, or until a toothpick inserted in the center comes out clean.

Remove the cake from the oven and let it cool in the skillet for 10 minutes. The skillet will still be hot. Cover a baking sheet with foil and invert it on top of the skillet. Wearing oven mitts, hold the edge of the sheet and the large handle of the skillet with one hand and use the other hand as a guide to keep the sheet and skillet together as you turn them over as a unit. Remove the skillet from the inverted cake, then use an offset spatula to slide the cake from the sheet to a large plate.

Let the cake cool, then serve topped with whipped cream, coconut gelato, toasted coconut, and pineapple chunks. A maraschino cherry on top makes it all the more festive!

chocolate
cakes

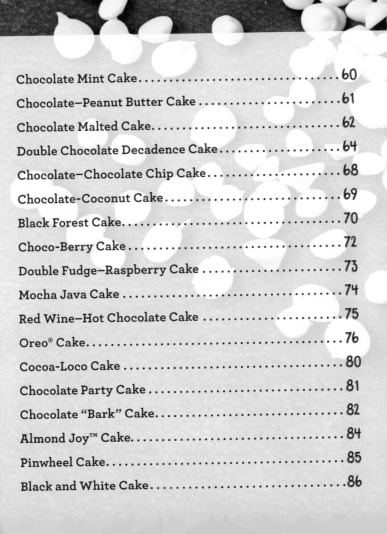

CHOCOLATE—THE WORD ITSELF makes me happy. Sometimes, there's just no substitute for chocolate, and if you ask me, nothing beats a rich chocolate cake. True, you can't get quite as experimental with chocolate as you can with vanilla, but there are certainly lots of flavors—peanut butter, coconut, raspberry, cookies, mint—that complement it, and even enhance it, including more chocolate! My goal in creating these dump cakes was to offer a variety of chocolate experiences that are really satisfying and keep the baking experience simple. I know that I tend to get cravings for chocolate cake late in the day or well after dinner, and I want to be able to throw something together that yields a delicious treat in an hour or less. Then again, I like to serve chocolate cakes to friends and bring them to parties, too. In those instances, it's nice to have recipes that are a bit more interesting, even if they require a bit more time. You'll find them all here. When you want chocolate cake, you should have lots of options.

chocolate mint cake

The pairing of chocolate and mint is a classic one, and there are many ways to enjoy it. I still had a box of Andes Thin Mints in my pantry after the holidays and thought I would use them instead of chocolate chips. The result was even better. If you want a restaurant look, you can add raspberries and fresh mint for a pretty garnish.

TIME: 1 hour

SERVES 8

3 tablespoons butter

28 Andes Thin Mints (one 4.67-ounce box), cut into pea-size pieces

1 box chocolate cake mix

2 tablespoons unsweetened cocoa powder

1 cup water

½ cup vegetable oil

6 ounces unsweetened applesauce

2 large eggs

Fresh raspberries, fresh mint, and mint chocolate chip ice cream, for serving (optional)

Preheat the oven to 350°F.

Melt the butter in a 12- or 12½-inch cast iron skillet over low heat while preparing the batter. Don't let the butter burn. If your burner has a very low setting, that's best. If the butter starts to brown, remove the skillet from the burner.

Put the candy pieces in a small bowl and dust with just enough cake mix to coat.

Combine the remaining cake mix, cocoa powder, water, oil, applesauce, and eggs in a large bowl and stir until well combined. Add the dusted candy pieces and stir until evenly distributed.

Pour the batter over the butter in the skillet.

Bake the cake for 35 minutes, or until a toothpick inserted in the center comes out clean.

Remove the cake from the oven and let it cool in the skillet for 10 minutes. The skillet will still be hot. Cover a baking sheet with foil and invert it on top of the skillet. Wearing oven mitts, hold the edge of the sheet and the large handle of the skillet with one hand and use the other hand as a guide to keep the sheet and skillet together as you turn them over as a unit. Remove the skillet from the inverted cake, then use an offset spatula to slide the cake from the sheet to a large plate.

Let the cake cool, then serve with the raspberries and mint, and maybe a scoop of mint chocolate chip ice cream for an over-the-top experience.

chocolate-peanut Butter cake

Do you love chocolate cake? Do you love any chocolate-peanut butter combination? If you answered yes to both of these questions, you will love, love, love this cake.

TIME: 1 hour

SERVES 8

2 tablespoons butter

1 box chocolate cake mix

2 large eggs

½ cup vegetable oil

6 ounces unsweetened applesauce

1 cup peanut butter chips

½ cup peanut butter (preferably all-natural and sugar-free)

Preheat the oven to 350°F.

Melt the butter in a 12- or 12½-inch cast iron skillet over low heat while preparing the batter. Don't let the butter burn. If the butter starts to brown, remove the skillet from the burner.

Combine the cake mix, eggs, oil, and applesauce in a large bowl and beat with an electric mixer or stir until smooth. Add the peanut butter chips and stir until well combined.

Put the peat butter in a small microwave-safe bowl and microwave on high until slightly warm and soft, about 30 seconds. Stir just until the ideal consistency for drizzling is reached (do not over-stir, or the peanut butter will separate).

Pour the batter over the butter in the skillet. Drizzle the melted peanut butter over the top.

Bake the cake for 35 to 45 minutes, or until a toothpick inserted in the center comes out clean.

Remove the cake from the oven and let it cool in the skillet for 10 minutes. The skillet will still be hot. Cover a baking sheet with foil and invert it on top of the skillet. Wearing oven mitts, hold the edge of the sheet and the large handle of the skillet with one hand and use the other hand as a guide to keep the sheet and skillet together as you turn them over as a unit. Remove the skillet from the inverted cake, then use an offset spatula to slide the cake from the sheet to a large plate.

Let the cake cool before serving.

chocolate malted cake

For fans of malted milk balls and malted chocolate shakes, here's a way to sass up your chocolate cake experience. You might even want to make an Ovaltine milk shake with vanilla ice cream to go along with it.

TIME: 1 hour

SERVES 8

3 tablespoons butter

1 box chocolate cake mix

2 tablespoons unsweetened cocoa powder

⅓ cup Rich Chocolate Ovaltine

1 cup water

½ cup vegetable oil

6 ounces unsweetened applesauce

3 large eggs

Chocolate ice cream, for serving (optional)

Preheat the oven to 350°F.

Melt the butter in a 12- or 12½-inch cast iron skillet over low heat while preparing the batter. Don't let the butter burn. If your burner has a very low setting, that's best. If the butter starts to brown, remove the skillet from the burner.

Combine the cake mix, cocoa powder, Ovaltine, water, oil, applesauce, and eggs in a large bowl and stir until well combined.

Pour the batter over the butter in the skillet.

Bake the cake for 35 minutes, or until a toothpick inserted in the center comes out clean.

Remove the cake from the oven and let it cool in the skillet for 10 minutes. The skillet will still be hot. Cover a baking sheet with foil and invert it on top of the skillet. Wearing oven mitts, hold the edge of the sheet and the large handle of the skillet with one hand and use the other hand as a guide to keep the sheet and skillet together as you turn them over as a unit. Remove the skillet from the inverted cake, then use an offset spatula to slide the cake from the sheet to a large plate.

Let the cake cool, then serve with chocolate ice cream.

Variation: *If you really love the flavor of chocolate malt, add some chocolate malted candies to the batter. Put about* ¾ **cup malted milk balls** *in a small bowl and dust with some of the cake mix. Prepare the batter as directed; after everything is thoroughly combined, gently stir in the dusted candies, being careful not to over-stir. Pour the batter into the skillet and bake as directed.*

Double Chocolate Decadence Cake

When you're in the mood for a fudgy, simple chocolate cake, look no further than this recipe. It's so easy to make and so good. Beware!

TIME: 1 hour

SERVES 8

6 tablespoons butter

1 cup semi-sweet or dark chocolate morsels

1 box chocolate cake mix

2 tablespoons unsweetened cocoa powder

1 cup water

½ cup vegetable oil

6 ounces unsweetened applesauce

3 large eggs

Chocolate sauce and raspberries and/or strawberries, for garnish (optional)

Preheat the oven to 350°F.

Melt the butter in a 12- or 12½-inch cast iron skillet over medium heat, then add ½ cup of the chocolate morsels and stir until melted. Keep warm over low heat while preparing the batter. If your burner has a very low setting, that's best. If the mixture starts to bubble, remove the skillet from the burner.

Put the remaining ½ cup chocolate morsels in a small bowl and dust with just enough cake mix to coat. Combine the remaining cake mix, cocoa powder, water, oil, applesauce, and eggs in a large bowl and stir until well combined. Stir in the coated morsels.

Pour the batter over the chocolate in the skillet.

Bake the cake for 35 to 40 minutes, or until a toothpick inserted in the center comes out clean.

Remove the cake from the oven and let it cool in the skillet for 10 minutes. The skillet will still be hot. Cover a baking sheet with foil and invert it on top of the skillet. Wearing oven mitts, hold the edge of the sheet and the large handle of the skillet with one hand and use the other hand as a guide to keep the sheet and skillet together as you turn them over as a unit. Remove the skillet from the inverted cake, then use an offset spatula to slide the cake from the sheet to a large plate.

Let the cake cool, then drizzle the top with chocolate sauce and garnish with raspberries and/or strawberries.

chocolate-chocolate chip cake

This is yet another take on a double-chocolate cake, and why not? In fact, all types of chocolate chips work here, even a combination. (It's a great way to use up extra chocolate chips or even pieces of chocolate candy that you might have in your pantry.)

TIME: 1 hour

SERVES 8

2 tablespoons butter

1 box chocolate cake mix

2 large eggs

½ cup vegetable oil

6 ounces unsweetened applesauce

1 cup chocolate chips (semi-sweet, dark, white, or a combination)

Vanilla ice cream or whipped cream and chocolate sauce, for serving (optional)

Preheat the oven to 350°F.

Melt the butter in a 12- or 12½-inch cast iron skillet over low heat while preparing the batter. Don't let the butter burn. If your burner has a very low setting, that's best. If the butter starts to brown, remove the skillet from the burner.

Combine the cake mix, eggs, oil, and applesauce in a large bowl and beat with an electric mixer or stir until smooth. Add the chocolate chips and stir until well combined.

Pour the cake batter over the butter in the skillet.

Bake the cake for 35 to 45 minutes, or until a toothpick inserted in the center comes out clean.

Remove the cake from the oven and let it cool in the skillet for 10 minutes. The skillet will still be hot. Cover a baking sheet with foil and invert it on top of the skillet. Wearing oven mitts, hold the edge of the sheet and the large handle of the skillet with one hand and use the other hand as a guide to keep the sheet and skillet together as you turn them over as a unit. Remove the skillet from the inverted cake, then use an offset spatula to slide the cake from the sheet to a large plate.

Let the cake cool, then serve with vanilla ice cream or fresh whipped cream, and drizzle with chocolate sauce.

chocolate-coconut cake

Here's another killer flavor combination: chocolate and coconut. They are heavenly together! In this recipe, vegetable oil is replaced with coconut oil, which doesn't tip the flavor scale but adds another coconut dimension to the coconut cream and flaked coconut in the cake.

TIME: 1 hour

SERVES 8

2 tablespoons butter

1 box chocolate cake mix

2 tablespoons unsweetened cocoa powder

½ cup coconut oil, melted

¾ cup coconut cream

6 ounces unsweetened applesauce

2 large eggs

1½ cups unsweetened coconut flakes

Preheat the oven to 350°F.

Melt the butter in a 12- or 12½-inch cast iron skillet over low heat while preparing the batter. Don't let the butter burn. If your burner has a very low setting, that's best. If the butter starts to brown, remove the skillet from the burner.

Combine the cake mix, cocoa powder, coconut oil, coconut cream, applesauce, and eggs in a large bowl and beat with an electric mixer or stir until smooth. Stir in 1 cup of the coconut flakes.

Pour the batter over the butter in the skillet.

Bake the cake for 35 to 45 minutes, or until a toothpick inserted in the center comes out clean.

Remove the cake from the oven and let it cool in the skillet for 10 minutes. The skillet will still be hot. Cover a baking sheet with foil and invert it on top of the skillet. Wearing oven mitts, hold the edge of the sheet and the large handle of the skillet with one hand and use the other hand as a guide to keep the sheet and skillet together as you turn them over as a unit. Remove the skillet from the inverted cake, then use an offset spatula to slide the cake from the sheet to a large plate.

Let the cake cool, then sprinkle with the remaining ½ cup coconut flakes.

Black Forest Cake

Germany has a sweet tooth, and one of its notable achievements is the Black Forest Cake, also known as Schwarzwälder Kirschtorte, made with chocolate sponge cake and a cherry and whipped cream filling and topping. As you may have guessed by the German name, kirsch (the sour cherry brandy) is included, too. I decided not to use kirsch here, but if you're so inspired, see the Variation, right. Kirsch or no, the chocolate-cherry flavor combination of this heavenly cake is deeply satisfying.

TIME: 1 hour

SERVES 8

2 tablespoons butter

1 box Devil's Food chocolate cake mix

12 ounces (1½ cups) black cherry soda

1 (20-ounce) can cherry pie filling

Sweetened whipped cream and maraschino cherries, for serving (optional)

Preheat the oven to 350°F.

Melt the butter in a 12- or 12½-inch cast iron skillet over low heat while preparing the batter. Don't let the butter burn. If your burner has a very low setting, that's best. If the butter starts to brown, remove the skillet from the burner.

Combine the cake mix and soda in a large bowl and stir until smooth. Add the cherry pie filling and stir until just combined.

Pour the batter over the butter in the skillet.

Bake the cake for 40 to 45 minutes, or until a toothpick inserted in the center comes out clean.

Remove the cake from the oven and let it cool in the skillet for 10 minutes. The skillet will still be hot. Cover a baking sheet with foil and invert it on top of the skillet. Wearing oven mitts, hold the edge of the sheet and the large handle of the skillet with one hand and use the other hand as a guide to keep the sheet and skillet together as you turn them over as a unit. Remove the skillet from the inverted cake, then use an offset spatula to slide the cake from the sheet to a large plate.

Let the cake cool, then serve with a generous amount of fresh sweetened whipped cream and maraschino cherries.

Variation: *To mimic the authentic German Black Forest Cake, stir a couple of tablespoons of* **kirsch (cherry brandy)** *into the melted butter in the skillet before the batter is added. This will add an intense cherry flavor, and it will also give a crusty cherry topping to the cake.*

Choco-Berry Cake

Chocolate cake studded with summer fruits and finished with a blast of strawberry jam! You'll want to keep this one in mind for al fresco meals on the patio. With fresh fruit on the side, it says summer. Luckily, this cake can be made successfully with frozen berries, too, so you can enjoy it year-round.

TIME: 1 hour

SERVES 8

2 tablespoons butter

1 box chocolate cake mix

2 tablespoons unsweetened cocoa powder

1 cup water

½ cup vegetable oil

6 ounces unsweetened applesauce

2 large eggs

¾ cup blueberries (preferably fresh)

1 cup strawberries, sliced thin or cut into pieces (preferably fresh)

½ cup strawberry jam

Fresh fruit, for serving (optional)

Preheat the oven to 350°F.

Melt the butter in a 12- or 12½-inch cast iron skillet over low heat while preparing the batter. Don't let the butter burn. If the butter starts to brown, remove the skillet from the burner.

Combine the cake mix, cocoa powder, water, oil, applesauce, and eggs in a large bowl and beat with an electric mixer or stir until smooth. Add the blueberries and stir until just combined.

Pour the batter over the butter in the skillet. Arrange the strawberry slices or pieces evenly over the top, and gently press them into the batter.

Put the strawberry jam in a microwave-safe bowl and microwave on high for 20 to 30 seconds, or until the jam is just melted, then drizzle over the cake.

Bake the cake for 35 to 45 minutes, or until a toothpick inserted in the center comes out clean.

Remove the cake from the oven and let it cool in the skillet for 10 minutes. The skillet will still be hot. Cover a baking sheet with foil and invert it on top of the skillet. Wearing oven mitts, hold the edge of the sheet and the large handle of the skillet with one hand and use the other hand as a guide to keep the sheet and skillet together as you turn them over as a unit. Remove the skillet from the inverted cake, then use an offset spatula to slide the cake from the sheet to a large plate.

Let the cake cool, then serve with more fresh fruit.

Double Fudge-Raspberry Cake

Chocolate, chocolate, chocolate, and then some raspberry. This cake is gooey and fudgy and irresistible. Offer the kids a glass of milk and the adults an espresso, and you'll have some pretty happy folks at your table.

TIME: 1 hour

SERVES 8

2 tablespoons butter

1 box fudge cake mix

2 tablespoons unsweetened cocoa powder

2 large eggs

½ cup vegetable oil

6 ounces unsweetened applesauce

½ cup raspberry jam

½ cup chocolate syrup

Fresh raspberries, for topping the cake

Preheat the oven to 350°F.

Melt the butter in a 12- or 12½-inch cast iron skillet over low heat while preparing the batter. Don't let the butter burn. If your burner has a very low setting, that's best. If the butter starts to brown, remove the skillet from the burner.

Combine the cake mix, cocoa powder, eggs, oil, and applesauce in a large bowl and beat with an electric mixer or stir until smooth.

Pour the batter over the butter in the skillet.

Put the raspberry jam in a microwave-safe bowl and microwave on high for 20 to 30 seconds, or until just melted. Stir in the chocolate syrup and drizzle the sauce over the batter.

Bake the cake for 35 to 45 minutes, or until a toothpick inserted in the center comes out clean.

Remove the cake from the oven and let it cool in the skillet for 10 minutes. The skillet will still be hot. Cover a baking sheet with foil and invert it on top of the skillet. Wearing oven mitts, hold the edge of the sheet and the large handle of the skillet with one hand and use the other hand as a guide to keep the sheet and skillet together as you turn them over as a unit. Remove the skillet from the inverted cake, then use an offset spatula to slide the cake from the sheet to a large plate.

Let the cake cool, then arrange plenty of raspberries on top and serve.

mocha Java Cake

For years and years when I lived and worked in New York City, I treated myself to a mocha java coffee almost every afternoon. Not only was it an energy boost, it was a midday dessert! This cake recaptures that same fabulous taste, and it provides that often-needed jolt of energy, too.

TIME: 1 hour

SERVES 8

2 tablespoons butter

1 box chocolate cake mix

2 tablespoons unsweetened cocoa powder

2 large eggs

½ cup vegetable oil

1 cup brewed espresso coffee, cold

½ cup chocolate-covered coffee beans (optional)

Coffee ice cream, chocolate sauce, and whipped cream, for serving (optional)

Preheat the oven to 350°F.

Melt the butter in a 12- or 12½-inch cast iron skillet over low heat while preparing the batter. Don't let the butter burn. If your burner has a very low setting, that's best. If the butter starts to brown, remove the skillet from the burner.

Combine the cake mix, cocoa powder, eggs, oil, and espresso in a large bowl and beat with an electric mixer or stir until smooth.

Pour the batter over the butter in the skillet, then sprinkle the coffee beans, if using, evenly over the top.

Bake the cake for 35 to 40 minutes, or until a toothpick inserted in the center comes out clean.

Remove the cake from the oven and let it cool in the skillet for 10 minutes. The skillet will still be hot. Cover a baking sheet with foil and invert it on top of the skillet. Wearing oven mitts, hold the edge of the sheet and the large handle of the skillet with one hand and use the other hand as a guide to keep the sheet and skillet together as you turn them over as a unit. Remove the skillet from the inverted cake, then use an offset spatula to slide the cake from the sheet to a large plate.

Let the cake cool, then serve with coffee ice cream, chocolate syrup . . . and whipped cream, too!

Red Wine-
Hot Chocolate Cake

On a lazy afternoon in the dead of winter, when it gets dark so early, there's nothing better than a mug of hot chocolate with a good glug of red wine added for good measure (okay, and maybe some whipped cream to top it off). The wine adds an earthiness, along with a gentle buzz, that is just right for a snooze in front of the fire. The wine that's baked into this cake won't affect you, as the alcohol will be cooked away, but the taste will be there.

TIME: 1 hour

SERVES 8

2 tablespoons butter

1 box chocolate cake mix

2 tablespoons hot chocolate mix

1 cup light- or medium-bodied red wine (such as Pinot Noir or Merlot)

½ cup vegetable oil

2 large eggs

Cabernet Sauvignon or Malbec, for serving (optional)

Preheat the oven to 350°F.

Melt the butter in a 12- or 12½-inch cast iron skillet over low heat while preparing the batter. Don't let the butter burn. If your burner has a very low setting, that's best. If the butter starts to brown, remove the skillet from the burner.

Combine the cake mix, hot chocolate mix, wine, oil, and eggs in a large bowl and beat with an electric mixer or stir until smooth.

Pour the batter over the butter in the skillet.

Bake the cake for 30 to 40 minutes, or until a toothpick inserted in the center comes out clean.

Remove the cake from the oven and let it cool in the skillet for 10 minutes. The skillet will still be hot. Cover a baking sheet with foil and invert it on top of the skillet. Wearing oven mitts, hold the edge of the sheet and the large handle of the skillet with one hand and use the other hand as a guide to keep the sheet and skillet together as you turn them over as a unit. Remove the skillet from the inverted cake, then use an offset spatula to slide the cake from the sheet to a large plate.

Let the cake cool before serving. A glass of full-bodied red wine, like a Cabernet Sauvignon or Malbec, is just the ticket with this dessert.

Oreo Cake

I like to make "cookie dump cakes" whenever I get a craving for something cake-y and chocolate-y and want something fast. All it takes is the cake mix, ingredients called for on the box, and a bunch of crushed cookies. Oreos are a good choice because they are intensely chocolate and hold up well through the baking. (For other cookie options, see Variation, right.)

TIME: 1 hour

SERVES 8

2 tablespoons butter

1 box chocolate cake mix

2 large eggs

½ cup vegetable oil

6 ounces unsweetened applesauce

1½ cups crushed Oreo cookie pieces (not too big but not pulverized, either)

Chocolate ice cream, for serving (optional)

Preheat the oven to 350°F.

Melt the butter in a 12- or 12½-inch cast iron skillet over low heat while preparing the batter. Don't let the butter burn. If your burner has a very low setting, that's best. If the butter starts to brown, remove the skillet from the burner.

Combine the cake mix, eggs, oil, and applesauce in a large bowl and beat with an electric mixer or stir until smooth.

Pour the batter over the butter in the skillet. Sprinkle the cookie pieces evenly over the top, then gently push the pieces into the batter.

Bake the cake for 35 to 45 minutes, or until a toothpick inserted in the center comes out clean.

Remove the cake from the oven and let it cool in the skillet for 10 minutes. The skillet will still be hot. Cover a baking sheet with foil and invert it on top of the skillet. Wearing oven mitts, hold the edge of the sheet and the large handle of the skillet with one hand and use the other hand as a guide to keep the sheet and skillet together as you turn them over as a unit. Remove the skillet from the inverted cake, then use an offset spatula to slide the cake from the sheet to a large plate.

Let the cake cool, then serve warm with ice cream.

Variation: *You can use different types of cookie pieces to take your chocolate cake in a different flavor direction. Try* **chocolate chip cookies, Pepperidge Farm® Mint Milano® cookies,** *or even* **ginger snaps.** *They are all terrific!*

Cocoa-Loco Cake

Everyone who knows me knows that I like hot sauce. A lot. I put it on almost everything. So, I was delighted when confectioners started adding everything from cayenne to wasabi to ginger to their chocolates for a blast of heat. This cake delivers the chocolate/heat pairing—big time.

TIME: 1 hour

SERVES 8

3 tablespoons butter

1 box chocolate fudge cake mix

1 teaspoon cinnamon

1 teaspoon cayenne pepper

1 teaspoon freshly ground black pepper

3 large eggs

½ cup vegetable oil

6 ounces unsweetened applesauce

¼ teaspoon vanilla extract

½ cup semi-sweet chocolate chips

Whipped cream and a shot of Fireball (or other cinnamon liqueur), for serving (optional)

Preheat the oven to 350°F.

Melt the butter in a 12- or 12½-inch cast iron skillet over low heat while preparing the batter. Don't let the butter burn. If your burner has a very low setting, that's best. If the butter starts to brown, remove the skillet from the burner.

Combine the cake mix, cinnamon, cayenne pepper, black pepper, eggs, oil, applesauce, and vanilla extract in a large bowl and beat with an electric mixer or stir until smooth.

Pour the batter over the butter in the skillet and sprinkle the chocolate chips evenly over the top.

Bake the cake for 30 to 40 minutes, or until a toothpick inserted in the center comes out clean.

Remove the cake from the oven and let it cool in the skillet for 10 minutes. The skillet will still be hot. Cover a baking sheet with foil and invert it on top of the skillet. Wearing oven mitts, hold the edge of the sheet and the large handle of the skillet with one hand and use the other hand as a guide to keep the sheet and skillet together as you turn them over as a unit. Remove the skillet from the inverted cake, then use an offset spatula to slide the cake from the sheet to a large plate.

Let the cake cool, then serve with whipped cream and a shot of Fireball or other cinnamon liqueur.

chocolate party cake

Cutting into a cake speckled with mini M&M's is fun, there's no doubt about it. This is the perfect recipe for a school night, when you want an easy dessert that can also be packed in the kids' lunchboxes the next day.

TIME: 1 hour

SERVES 8

2 tablespoons butter

1 box chocolate cake mix

3 large eggs

½ cup vegetable oil

6 ounces unsweetened applesauce

1 cup mini M&M's pieces

1 to 2 tablespoons flour

Ice cream, for serving (optional)

Preheat the oven to 350°F.

Melt the butter in a 12- or 12½-inch cast iron skillet over low heat while preparing the batter. Don't let the butter burn. If your burner has a very low setting, that's best. If the butter starts to brown, remove the skillet from the burner.

Combine the cake mix, eggs, oil, and applesauce in a large bowl and beat with an electric mixer or stir until smooth. Put the mini M&M's in a small bowl and dust with just enough flour to coat. Add the coated candy to the batter and stir until just combined.

Pour the batter over the butter in the skillet.

Bake the cake for 35 to 40 minutes, or until a toothpick inserted in the center comes out clean.

Remove the cake from the oven and let it cool in the skillet for 10 minutes. The skillet will still be hot. Cover a baking sheet with foil and invert it on top of the skillet. Wearing oven mitts, hold the edge of the sheet and the large handle of the skillet with one hand and use the other hand as a guide to keep the sheet and skillet together as you turn them over as a unit. Remove the skillet from the inverted cake, then use an offset spatula to slide the cake from the sheet to a large plate.

Let the cake cool, then serve with ice cream.

chocolate "Bark" cake

Traditionally, chocolate bark is a combination of dark chocolate, white chocolate, and peppermint. If these flavors work well together as a candy—and they do—they certainly work well together as a cake.

TIME: 1 hour

SERVES 8

2 tablespoons butter

1 box chocolate fudge cake mix

3 large eggs

½ cup vegetable oil

1 cup water

½ teaspoon peppermint extract

½ cup crushed peppermint pinwheel candies

Chocolate ice cream, for serving (optional)

Preheat the oven to 350°F.

Melt the butter in a 12- or 12½-inch cast iron skillet over low heat while preparing the batter. Don't let the butter burn. If your burner has a very low setting, that's best. If the butter starts to brown, remove the skillet from the burner.

Combine the cake mix, eggs, oil, water, and peppermint extract in a large bowl and beat with an electric mixer or stir until smooth.

Pour the batter over the butter in the skillet. Sprinkle the peppermint candy pieces evenly over the top.

Bake the cake for 35 to 45 minutes, or until a toothpick inserted in the center comes out clean.

Remove the cake from the oven and let it cool in the skillet for 10 minutes. The skillet will still be hot. Cover a baking sheet with foil and invert it on top of the skillet. Wearing oven mitts, hold the edge of the sheet and the large handle of the skillet with one hand and use the other hand as a guide to keep the sheet and skillet together as you turn them over as a unit. Remove the skillet from the inverted cake, then use an offset spatula to slide the cake from the sheet to a large plate.

Let the cake cool, then serve with chocolate ice cream.

Variation: *You can make cupcakes instead of a full skillet cake with any of the batters in this book, but bark cupcakes are a special treat for everyone, especially when paired with a sweet, minty, and creamy frosting. To make the cupcakes, line a cupcake tin with paper wrappers and pour enough batter to fill the tins two-thirds full. Bake the cupcakes at 350°F for about 20 minutes, or until a tester comes out clean. For the frosting: Cream together ½* **cup (1 stick) butter**, **1 cup confectioners' sugar**, *and* **1 teaspoon peppermint extract** *in a bowl until creamy. When the cupcakes are cool, frost them and sprinkle the tops with crushed peppermint candies.*

almond Joy Cake

Do you remember the jingle for Almond Joy candy back in the 1970s? "Sometimes you feel like a nut/Sometimes you don't/Almond Joy's got nuts/Mounds don't." Not only do I remember it, I used to sing along because I often felt like a nut (enjoying one, that is), and I loved Almond Joy candy bars. Clearly, I still do.

TIME: 1 hour

SERVES 8

2 tablespoons butter

1 box chocolate fudge cake mix

2 large eggs

½ cup vegetable oil

1 cup water

8 to 10 mini Almond Joy™ candy bars, or larger bars cut into 1-inch pieces to yield about ¾ cup

Coconut ice cream, for serving (optional)

Preheat the oven to 350°F.

Melt the butter in a 12- or 12½-inch cast iron skillet over low heat while preparing the batter. Don't let the butter burn. If your burner has a very low setting, that's best. If the butter starts to brown, remove the skillet from the burner.

Combine the cake mix, eggs, oil, and water in a large bowl and beat with an electric mixer or stir until smooth.

Pour the batter over the butter in the skillet. Arrange the mini candy bars or candy pieces evenly in the skillet, leaving plenty of room around the pieces for the cake to expand while baking.

Bake the cake for 40 minutes, or until a toothpick inserted in the center comes out clean.

Remove the cake from the oven and let it cool in the skillet for 10 minutes. The skillet will still be hot. Cover a baking sheet with foil and invert it on top of the skillet. Wearing oven mitts, hold the edge of the sheet and the large handle of the skillet with one hand and use the other hand as a guide to keep the sheet and skillet together as you turn them over as a unit. Remove the skillet from the inverted cake, then use an offset spatula to slide the cake from the sheet to a large plate.

Let the cake cool, then serve with coconut ice cream.

pinwheel cake

Ah, Pinwheel cookies! Remember them from your childhood? The ones with a crumbly cookie base that's topped with a puff of marshmallow and then covered in a shell of silky chocolate? I love all the different textures you get in one bite! My goal here was to incorporate a cookie into a cake that would keep its same consistency after baking. And, as it turns out, Pinwheels and chocolate cake are great partners.

TIME: 1 hour

SERVES 7

2 tablespoons butter

1 tablespoon coffee liqueur (optional)

1 box chocolate fudge cake mix

2 large eggs

½ cup vegetable oil

1 cup water

7 Pinwheel cookies

Chocolate or coffee ice cream, for serving (optional)

Preheat the oven to 350°F.

Melt the butter in a 12- or 12½-inch cast iron skillet over low heat, then add the coffee liqueur, if using, and swirl around to combine with the butter. Keep warm over low heat while preparing the batter. If the butter starts to brown, remove the skillet from the burner.

Combine the cake mix, eggs, oil, and water in a large bowl and beat with an electric mixer or stir until smooth.

Pour the batter over the coffee liqueur/butter mixture in the skillet. Arrange six of the Pinwheel cookies upside-down in a circle near the center of the batter, leaving enough room to place the remaining cookie, also upside-down, in the very center. Press the cookies gently into the batter.

Bake the cake for 40 minutes, or until a toothpick inserted near the center comes out clean.

Remove the cake from the oven and let it cool in the skillet for 10 minutes. The skillet will still be hot. Cover a baking sheet with foil and invert it on top of the skillet. Wearing oven mitts, hold the edge of the sheet and the large handle of the skillet with one hand and use the other hand as a guide to keep the sheet and skillet together as you turn them over as a unit. Remove the skillet from the inverted cake, then use an offset spatula to slide the cake from the sheet to a large plate.

Let the cake cool, then serve with chocolate or coffee ice cream.

Black and White Cake

This chocolate cake, loaded with white chocolate chips, produces a whimsical polka-dot dessert. Keep this one in mind for a fun get-together—not only is it fun to look at, it's tasty, too.

TIME: 1 hour

SERVES 8

2 tablespoons butter

2 tablespoons chocolate liqueur (optional)

1 box chocolate cake mix

2 large eggs

½ cup vegetable oil

6 ounces unsweetened applesauce

1½ cups white chocolate chips

1 to 2 tablespoons flour

Vanilla ice cream, for serving (optional)

Preheat the oven to 350°F.

Melt the butter in a 12- or 12½-inch cast iron skillet over low heat, then stir in the chocolate liqueur, if using, and keep warm on very low heat while preparing the batter. Don't let the butter burn. If your burner has a very low setting, that's best. If the butter starts to brown, remove the skillet from the burner.

Combine the cake mix, eggs, oil, and applesauce in a large bowl and beat with an electric mixer or stir until smooth. Put 1 cup of the white chocolate chips in a small bowl and dust with just enough flour to coat. Add the coated chips to the batter and stir until just combined.

Pour the batter over the butter and chocolate liqueur in the skillet. Sprinkle the remaining ½ cup white chocolate chips evenly over the top.

Bake the cake for 35 to 45 minutes, or until a toothpick inserted in the center comes out clean.

Remove the cake from the oven and let it cool in the skillet for 10 minutes. The skillet will still be hot. Cover a baking sheet with foil and invert it on top of the skillet. Wearing oven mitts, hold the edge of the sheet and the large handle of the skillet with one hand and use the other hand as a guide to keep the sheet and skillet together as you turn them over as a unit. Remove the skillet from the inverted cake, then use an offset spatula to slide the cake from the sheet to a large plate.

Let the cake cool, then serve with ice cream.

carrot cakes

A **REALLY GOOD CARROT CAKE**—loaded with bits of carrots, nuts, and just the right spices and frosted with cream cheese icing—is about as perfect as a dessert can be. My mouth waters just thinking about it! When you use a carrot cake mix, you're not getting homemade, but it provides a flavor mix that you can play with to create some of the tastiest cakes. Simply adding grated carrots and pineapple pieces or flaked coconut—even a few exotic spices—can make for some killer cakes. You don't have to frost these cakes, as they are perfectly fine on their own, but if you want to make a bowl of cream cheese frosting, I say go for it.

killer carrot cake

Whenever you have a hankering for a traditional carrot cake but don't have the time to make one, this cake will more than satisfy. It contains all the goodies that make carrot cake so moist and flavorful—carrots (of course), coconut, and pineapple. One bite, and you'll know why it's named "killer."

TIME: 1 hour

SERVES 8

½ cup canned pineapple chunks, plus ½ cup reserved juice from the can

½ cup unsweetened coconut flakes

1 box carrot cake mix

4 tablespoons butter

2 carrots, peeled and grated

⅓ cup vegetable oil

6 ounces unsweetened applesauce

3 large eggs

Fresh whipped cream and confectioners' sugar, for serving (optional)

Preheat the oven to 350°F.

Stir together the pineapple pieces (without the juice) and coconut flakes in a small bowl and dust with just enough cake mix to coat.

Melt the butter in a 12- or 12½-inch cast iron skillet over medium heat, then add the carrots, stirring until combined. Bring to a simmer over low heat, then keep warm. If the butter starts to brown, remove the skillet from the burner.

Combine the remaining cake mix, oil, applesauce, eggs, and reserved pineapple juice in a large bowl and stir or beat with an electric mixer until combined. Fold the dusted pineapple and coconut flakes into the batter with a spatula until just blended, and pour the batter over the carrot mixture in skillet.

Bake the cake for 35 to 40 minutes, or until a toothpick inserted in the center comes out clean.

Remove the cake from the oven and let it cool in the skillet for 10 minutes. The skillet will still be hot. Cover a baking sheet with foil and invert it on top of the skillet. Wearing oven mitts, hold the edge of the sheet and the large handle of the skillet with one hand and use the other hand as a guide to keep the sheet and skillet together as you turn them over as a unit. Remove the skillet from the inverted cake, then use an offset spatula to slide the cake from the sheet to a large plate.

Let the cake cool. Serve with whipped cream and a dusting of confectioners' sugar.

Variation: *Because sometimes a carrot cake just needs cream cheese frosting, here is my killer cream cheese frosting recipe: First, soften* **8 ounces cream cheese**, *and cut* **½ cup (1 stick) butter** *into little pieces and let soften, too. Blend the cream cheese in a large bowl with an electric mixer on low speed until smooth. Add the pieces of butter, one by one, beating on low or medium speed until each piece is incorporated. Add* **1 cup confectioners' sugar** *and beat on medium speed until just combined. Finally, add* **1 teaspoon vanilla extract** *and continue to beat until the frosting is well blended and creamy. Once the cake is cool, frost and refrigerate until ready to serve.*

granola carrot cake

While experimenting with boxed carrot cake mix, I found that it pairs really well with vanilla-almond granola. Another inspiration was to stir in some apple butter; it gently boosts the cinnamon, nutmeg, and clove flavors and adds plenty of moisture to the cake.

TIME: 1 hour

SERVES 8

2 tablespoons butter

½ cup vanilla-almond granola, or any granola of your choice

1 box carrot cake mix

⅛ cup whole flax seeds

6 ounces unsweetened applesauce

3 large eggs

⅓ cup vegetable oil

⅓ cup apple butter

Whipped cream or ice cream, for serving (optional)

Preheat the oven to 350°F.

Melt the butter in a 12- or 12½-inch cast iron skillet over low heat. Sprinkle the granola evenly over the butter and keep warm on low heat while preparing the batter.

Combine the cake mix, flax seeds, applesauce, eggs, oil, and apple butter in a large bowl and beat with an electric mixer or stir until smooth. Don't over-mix.

Pour the batter over the granola in the skillet.

Bake the cake for 40 minutes, or until a toothpick inserted in the center comes out clean.

Remove the cake from the oven and let it cool in the skillet for 10 minutes. The skillet will still be hot. Cover a baking sheet with foil and invert it on top of the skillet. Wearing oven mitts, hold the edge of the sheet and the large handle of the skillet with one hand and use the other hand as a guide to keep the sheet and skillet together as you turn them over as a unit. Remove the skillet from the inverted cake, then use an offset spatula to slide the cake from the sheet to a large plate.

Let the cake cool, then serve with whipped cream or ice cream.

pumpkin carrot cake

While you can't really consider cake a healthy food, orange veggies, like pumpkins and carrots, are filled with the powerful antioxidant carotenoid, so adding puréed pumpkin to this recipe certainly boosts its nutritional value. Of course, pumpkin adds wonderful color and flavor, too.

TIME: 1 hour

SERVES 8

2 tablespoons butter

1 box carrot cake mix

6 ounces unsweetened applesauce

3 large eggs

½ cup vegetable oil

¾ cup 100% pumpkin purée

1 tablespoon lemon juice

½ teaspoon ground ginger

½ teaspoon ground nutmeg

½ teaspoon ground cinnamon

Whipped cream or ice cream, for serving (optional)

Preheat the oven to 350°F.

Melt the butter in a 12- or 12½-inch cast iron skillet over low heat while preparing the batter. Don't let the butter burn. If your burner has a very low setting, that's best. If the butter starts to brown, remove the skillet from the burner.

Combine the cake mix, applesauce, eggs, oil, pumpkin purée, lemon juice, ginger, nutmeg, and cinnamon in a large bowl and beat with an electric mixer or stir until smooth.

Pour the batter over the butter in the skillet.

Bake the cake for 40 minutes, or until a toothpick inserted in the center comes out clean.

Remove the cake from the oven and let it cool in the skillet for 10 minutes. The skillet will still be hot. Cover a baking sheet with foil and invert it on top of the skillet. Wearing oven mitts, hold the edge of the sheet and the large handle of the skillet with one hand and use the other hand as a guide to keep the sheet and skillet together as you turn them over as a unit. Remove the skillet from the inverted cake, then use an offset spatula to slide the cake from the sheet to a large plate.

Let the cake cool, then serve with whipped cream or ice cream.

Morning Glory Cake

Loaded with pieces of apples, carrots, pineapple, and walnuts, this cake has lots of flavors and textures. I always loved morning glory muffins for their density and hints of savory flavors that complemented the sweetness inherent in the recipe. This cake comes close to replicating a delicious (and nutritious) morning glory muffin.

TIME: 1 hour

SERVES 8

1 small, firm apple, such as Macoun or Golden Delicious, cored, peeled, and cut into pebble-size pieces

2 carrots, peeled and finely grated

⅓ cup walnut pieces, crushed

1 box carrot cake mix

2 tablespoons butter

2 tablespoons dark brown sugar

3 large eggs

½ cup vegetable oil

½ teaspoon ground cinnamon

½ teaspoon ground nutmeg

6 ounces canned crushed pineapple, including the juice

Additional chopped apples, crushed pineapple, and walnuts, for garnish (optional)

Whipped cream, for serving (optional)

Preheat the oven to 350°F.

Combine the apple, carrots, and walnuts in a large bowl. Sprinkle about ¼ cup of the cake mix over the mixture and stir until coated.

Melt the butter in a 12- or 12½-inch cast iron skillet over low heat, then sprinkle the brown sugar evenly over the butter and keep warm. Don't let the mixture burn. If the mixture starts to brown, remove the skillet from the burner.

Combine the remaining cake mix, eggs, oil, cinnamon, and nutmeg in a large bowl and beat with an electric mixer or stir until smooth. Stir in the pineapple and juice, then gently fold the apple, carrot, and walnut mixture into the batter.

Pour the batter over the sugar mixture in the skillet.

Bake the cake for 40 minutes, or until a toothpick inserted in the center comes out clean.

Remove the cake from the oven and let it cool in the skillet for 10 minutes. The skillet will still be hot. Cover a baking sheet with foil and invert it on top of the skillet. Wearing oven mitts, hold the edge of the sheet and the large handle of the skillet with one hand and use the other hand as a guide to keep the sheet and skillet together as you turn them over as a unit. Remove the skillet from the inverted cake, then use an offset spatula to slide the cake from the sheet to a large plate.

Let the cake cool, then garnish with additional fruit and walnuts and serve with whipped cream.

carrot-cream cheesecake

If you are missing the classic cream cheese topping on these simple no-frosting carrot dump cakes, this recipe makes it all up to you (without having to make the frosting). I put the cream cheese in the batter, and yes, it works!

TIME: 1 hour

SERVES 8

2 tablespoons butter

2 tablespoons light brown sugar

1 box carrot cake mix

6 ounces unsweetened applesauce

2 large eggs

½ cup vegetable oil

1 teaspoon vanilla extract

4 ounces cream cheese

Confectioners' sugar, for garnish (optional)

Preheat the oven to 350°F.

Melt the butter in a 12- or 12½-inch cast iron skillet over low heat, then sprinkle the brown sugar evenly over the butter and keep warm over low heat while preparing the batter. Don't let the mixture burn. If your burner has a very low setting, that's best. If the mixture starts to get too brown, remove the skillet from the burner.

Combine the cake mix, applesauce, eggs, oil, and vanilla extract in a large bowl and beat with an electric mixer or stir until smooth. Put the cream cheese in a microwave-safe bowl and microwave on high for 20 to 30 seconds, or until just soft, then stir until smooth.

Pour the batter over the sugar mixture in the skillet. Drizzle the cream cheese evenly over the top.

Bake for 35 to 40 minutes, or until a toothpick inserted in the center comes out clean.

Remove the cake from the oven and let it cool in the skillet for 10 minutes. The skillet will still be hot. Cover a baking sheet with foil and invert it on top of the skillet. Wearing oven mitts, hold the edge of the sheet and the large handle of the skillet with one hand and use the other hand as a guide to keep the sheet and skillet together as you turn them over as a unit. Remove the skillet from the inverted cake, then use an offset spatula to slide the cake from the sheet to a large plate.

Let the cake cool completely, then dust with confectioners' sugar.

Lemony Carrot Cake

I love a pop of lemon in almost anything. It adds a brightness that is subtle but significant. You could even add another tablespoon here if you want more lemony flavor to come through.

TIME: 1 hour

SERVES 8

2 tablespoons butter

2 tablespoons light brown sugar

1 box instant lemon pudding mix

2 cups cold milk

1 box carrot cake mix

2 large eggs

⅓ cup vegetable oil

¼ cup fresh lemon juice

2 tablespoons lemon zest

Whipped cream or ice cream, for serving (optional)

Preheat the oven to 350°F.

Melt the butter in a 12- or 12½-inch cast iron skillet over low heat, then sprinkle the brown sugar evenly over the butter and keep warm on low heat while preparing the batter. Don't let the mixture burn. If your burner has a very low setting, that's best. If the mixture starts to brown, remove the skillet from the burner.

Combine the pudding mix and cold milk in a large bowl and whisk well until thickened, about 2 to 3 minutes. Add the cake mix, eggs, oil, lemon juice, and lemon zest and stir until smooth.

Pour the batter over the brown sugar mixture in the skillet.

Bake the cake for 35 to 40 minutes, or until a toothpick inserted in the center comes out clean.

Remove the cake from the oven and let it cool in the skillet for 10 minutes. The skillet will still be hot. Cover a baking sheet with foil and invert it on top of the skillet. Wearing oven mitts, hold the edge of the sheet and the large handle of the skillet with one hand and use the other hand as a guide to keep the sheet and skillet together as you turn them over as a unit. Remove the skillet from the inverted cake, then use an offset spatula to slide the cake from the sheet to a large plate.

Let the cake cool, then serve with whipped cream or ice cream.

carrot-pecan cake

Pecans have a mild sweet flavor that is a nice complement to carrot cake. The crushed nut pieces, coated with butter, form a yummy, crunchy topping when the cake is inverted. If you want to serve this cake (or any cake in this chapter) as an afternoon snack, see the Variation, right.

TIME: 1 hour

SERVES 8

2 tablespoons butter

1 cup pecan pieces, ½ cup crushed and ½ cup left whole

1 box carrot cake mix

6 ounces unsweetened applesauce

3 large eggs

½ cup vegetable oil

1 to 2 tablespoons flour

Whipped cream or ice cream, for serving (optional)

Preheat the oven to 350°F.

Melt the butter in a 12- or 12½-inch cast iron skillet over low heat, then sprinkle ½ cup crushed pecan pieces evenly over the butter and keep warm on low heat while preparing the batter.

Combine the cake mix, applesauce, eggs, and oil in a large bowl and beat with an electric mixer or stir until smooth. Put ½ cup whole pecan pieces in a small bowl and dust with just enough flour to coat. Fold the dusted pecan pieces into the cake batter.

Pour the batter over the crushed pecans in the skillet.

Bake the cake for 40 minutes, or until a toothpick inserted in the center comes out clean.

Remove the cake from the oven and let it cool in the skillet for 10 minutes. The skillet will still be hot. Cover a baking sheet with foil and invert it on top of the skillet. Wearing oven mitts, hold the edge of the sheet and the large handle of the skillet with one hand and use the other hand as a guide to keep the sheet and skillet together as you turn them over as a unit. Remove the skillet from the inverted cake, then use an offset spatula to slide the cake from the sheet to a large plate.

Let the cake cool, then serve with whipped cream or ice cream.

Variation: *For a perfect snack, you can serve slices of the cooled cake with a drizzle of a not-too-sweet confectioners' sugar and cream cheese glaze. To make the glaze: Put* **4 ounces (½ package) cream cheese, 1 cup confectioners' sugar, ½ cup milk (2%),** *and* **1 teaspoon vanilla extract** *in a bowl and beat with an electric mixer until creamy but not too thick. If necessary, add more milk by the tablespoon just until the right consistency for drizzling is reached.*

carrot-apple cake

Adding small pieces of peeled apple contributes taste and texture to this cake. I found that dusting the pieces with flour helps them "float" in the batter while baking. A drizzle of apple butter over the batter adds yet another layer of flavor that is baked into the cake.

TIME: 1 hour

SERVES 8

3 tablespoons butter

2 tablespoons dark brown sugar

1 box carrot cake mix

6 ounces unsweetened applesauce

3 large eggs

½ cup vegetable oil

½ teaspoon ground cinnamon

1 large, firm apple, like a Granny Smith or Macoun, cored, peeled, and cut into pebble-size pieces

1 or 2 tablespoons flour

⅓ cup apple butter

Whipped cream or ice cream, for serving (optional)

Preheat the oven to 350°F.

Melt the butter in a 12- or 12½-inch cast iron skillet over low heat, then sprinkle the brown sugar evenly over the butter and let it melt. Keep warm over low heat while preparing the batter. Don't let the sugar mixture burn. If your burner has a very low setting, that's best. If the butter starts to brown, remove the skillet from the burner.

Combine the cake mix, applesauce, eggs, oil, and cinnamon in a large bowl and beat with an electric mixer or stir until smooth. Put the apple pieces in a small bowl and dust with just enough flour to coat. Fold the dusted apple pieces into the batter.

Pour the batter over the brown sugar mixture in the skillet and drizzle the apple butter over the top.

Bake the cake for 40 minutes, or until a toothpick inserted in the center comes out clean.

Remove the cake from the oven and let it cool in the skillet for 10 minutes. The skillet will still be hot. Cover a baking sheet with foil and invert it on top of the skillet. Wearing oven mitts, hold the edge of the sheet and the large handle of the skillet with one hand and use the other hand as a guide to keep the sheet and skillet together as you turn them over as a unit. Remove the skillet from the inverted cake, then use an offset spatula to slide the cake from the sheet to a large plate.

Let the cake cool, then serve with whipped cream or ice cream.

Butterscotch Carrot Cake

The baking section of the grocery store is filled with all kinds of ingredients that you can add to your dump cakes, and butterscotch morsels should not be overlooked. I like them in a carrot cake, as their buttery flavor doesn't overwhelm the cake and adds a nice twist.

TIME: 1 hour

SERVES 8

2 tablespoons butter

1 box carrot cake mix

6 ounces unsweetened applesauce

3 large eggs

⅓ cup vegetable oil

½ teaspoon ground ginger

1 cup butterscotch morsels

1 to 2 tablespoons flour

Whipped cream or ice cream, for serving (optional)

Preheat the oven to 350°F.

Melt the butter in a 12- or 12½-inch cast iron skillet over low heat while preparing the batter. Don't let the butter burn. If your burner has a very low setting, that's best. If the butter starts to brown, remove the skillet from the burner.

Combine the cake mix, applesauce, eggs, oil, and ginger in a large bowl and beat with an electric mixer or stir until smooth. Don't over-mix. Put the butterscotch morsels in a bowl and dust with just enough flour to coat. Gently fold the morsels into the batter.

Pour the batter over the butter in the skillet.

Bake the cake for 40 minutes, or until a toothpick inserted in the center comes out clean.

Remove the cake from the oven and let it cool in the skillet for 10 minutes. The skillet will still be hot. Cover a baking sheet with foil and invert it on top of the skillet. Wearing oven mitts, hold the edge of the sheet and the large handle of the skillet with one hand and use the other hand as a guide to keep the sheet and skillet together as you turn them over as a unit. Remove the skillet from the inverted cake, then use an offset spatula to slide the cake from the sheet to a large plate.

Let the cake cool, then serve with whipped cream or ice cream.

Spice Cakes

'M GUESSING THAT MANY OF YOU have never made a spice cake from a boxed mix. Perhaps some of you don't even know that such a mix is available, let alone that it can serve as the foundation for countless yummy spice dump cakes. If true, you are in for a wonderful surprise, especially if you like cinnamon. The boxed mix is flavored with cinnamon (it even has a cinnamon-y hue), so all the natural pairings of this spice can, and should, be considered. Earthy fruits, like apples and pumpkins, are natural add-ins, but tropical fruits, like bananas, are great, too. You'll find spice cake variations for all of these here. I even created a very adult Port Wine Spice Cake that is pretty amazing. And, because most kids like cinnamon (think cinnamon-topped applesauce and cinnamon toast), I included several kid-friendly cakes, like Spicy Nicey Cake and Cinnamon-Sugar Spice Cake, for after-school treats.

Spicy Nicey Cake

I gave this easy-to-make and ready-to-eat cake a funny name because it's a spice cake with a few healthy additions. Individually, applesauce, unsweetened coconut flakes, and flax seeds are known for their nutritional goodness, and they add so much flavor to this cake. There's even a yummy granola crust on top.

TIME: 1 hour

SERVES 8

3 tablespoons butter

1 cup granola

1 box spice cake mix

1½ cups water

6 ounces unsweetened applesauce

3 large eggs

1 cup unsweetened coconut flakes

¼ cup whole flax seeds

Preheat the oven to 350°F.

Melt the butter in a 12- or 12½-inch cast iron skillet over medium heat, then add the granola, stirring to coat with the butter. Keep warm over low heat while preparing the batter. Don't let the butter burn. If it starts to brown, remove the skillet from the burner.

Combine the cake mix, water, applesauce, eggs, coconut, and flax seeds in a large bowl and stir until combined.

Pour the batter over the granola in the skillet.

Bake the cake for 35 to 40 minutes, or until a toothpick inserted in the center comes out clean.

Remove the cake from the oven and let it cool in the skillet for 10 minutes. The skillet will still be hot. Cover a baking sheet with foil and invert it on top of the skillet. Wearing oven mitts, hold the edge of the sheet and the large handle of the skillet with one hand and use the other hand as a guide to keep the sheet and skillet together as you turn them over as a unit. Remove the skillet from the inverted cake, then use an offset spatula to slide the cake from the sheet to a large plate.

Let the cake cool before serving.

Cinnamon Sugar Spice Cake

When I was little, my mother would make us "cinnamon toast" (toast loaded up with butter, then sprinkled with cinnamon and sugar) on especially chilly days or whenever we had a cold. It always hit the spot. That is the exact flavor combo I aimed for in this homey cake.

TIME: 1 hour

SERVES 8

1½ teaspoons ground cinnamon

1 tablespoon granulated sugar

2 tablespoons butter

1 box spice cake mix

½ cup vegetable oil

6 ounces unsweetened applesauce

3 large eggs

½ cup water

Pumpkin or butter pecan ice cream, for serving
(optional)

Preheat the oven to 350°F.

Put 1 teaspoon of the cinnamon and the granulated sugar in a small bowl and stir until combined.

Melt the butter in in a 12- or 12½-inch cast iron skillet over low heat, then sprinkle the cinnamon-sugar over the butter and keep warm on low heat while preparing the batter. Don't let the mixture burn. If your burner has a very low setting, that's best. If the mixture starts to get too brown, remove the skillet from the burner.

Combine the cake mix, oil, applesauce, eggs, water, and the remaining ½ teaspoon cinnamon in a large bowl and beat with an electric mixer or stir until smooth.

Pour the batter over the cinnamon-sugar mixture in the skillet.

Bake the cake for 30 to 35 minutes, or until a toothpick inserted in the center comes out clean.

Remove the cake from the oven and let it cool in the skillet for 10 minutes. The skillet will still be hot. Cover a baking sheet with foil and invert it on top of the skillet. Wearing oven mitts, hold the edge of the sheet and the large handle of the skillet with one hand and use the other hand as a guide to keep the sheet and skillet together as you turn them over as a unit. Remove the skillet from the inverted cake, then use an offset spatula to slide the cake from the sheet to a large plate.

Let the cake cool, then serve with pumpkin or butter pecan ice cream.

almond cookie spice cake

If you're a fan of Amaretto (the Italian almond liqueur), you're going to love this cake. It's made with the Amaretto cookies that you can sometimes find in the cookie section of your grocery store or the ones that come in signature bright orange tins and boxes, typically found in Italian food shops.

TIME: 1 hour

SERVES 8

2 cups Amaretto cookies

4 tablespoons butter

1 box spice cake mix

½ cup vegetable oil

6 ounces unsweetened applesauce

3 large eggs

1 teaspoon almond extract

2 cups mini marshmallows

Whipped cream (spiked with Amaretto liqueur, if desired) or ice cream, for serving (optional)

Preheat the oven to 350°F.

Put the cookies in a sealable plastic bag and crush them with a rolling pin into pea-size pieces.

Melt the butter in a 12- or 12½-inch cast iron skillet over low heat, then sprinkle the crushed cookies evenly over the butter. Keep warm over low heat. If the butter starts to brown, remove the skillet from the burner.

Combine the cake mix, oil, applesauce, eggs, and almond extract in a large bowl and beat with an electric mixer or stir until smooth. The batter should be slightly thick.

Pour the batter over the crushed cookies in the skillet. Arrange the mini marshmallows evenly over the top, but not too close to the sides of the skillet.

Bake the cake for about 35 minutes, or until a toothpick inserted in the center comes out clean.

Remove the cake from the oven and let it cool in the skillet for 10 minutes. The skillet will still be hot. Cover a baking sheet with foil and invert it on top of the skillet. Wearing oven mitts, hold the edge of the sheet and the large handle of the skillet with one hand and use the other hand as a guide to keep the sheet and skillet together as you turn them over as a unit. Remove the skillet from the inverted cake, then use an offset spatula to slide the cake from the sheet to a large plate.

Let the cake cool, then serve with fresh whipped cream or ice cream.

Variation: *To increase the Amaretto flavor even more, you can add* **Amaretto liqueur** *to the whipped cream as you are whipping it (1 tablespoon per 8 ounces, or to your liking).*

Banana Spice Cake

Bananas are the perfect addition to a spice cake mix. They add flavor, fiber, and texture and complement the spice flavors nicely. When you don't want to make banana bread with those slightly over-ripe bananas, try this instead.

TIME: 1 hour

SERVES 8

2 tablespoons butter

2 tablespoons light brown sugar

1 box spice cake mix

½ cup vegetable oil

6 ounces unsweetened applesauce

3 large eggs

½ cup water

2 ripe bananas, mashed, plus 1 ripe banana, sliced into thin rounds

½ teaspoon ground nutmeg

Whipped cream or ice cream, for serving (optional)

Preheat the oven to 350°F.

Melt the butter in a 12- or 12½-inch cast iron skillet over low heat, then sprinkle the brown sugar evenly over the butter and keep warm on low heat while preparing the batter. Don't let the mixture burn. If your burner has a very low setting, that's best. If the mixture starts to get too brown, remove the skillet from the burner.

Combine the cake mix, oil, applesauce, eggs, water, 2 mashed bananas, and nutmeg in a large bowl and beat with an electric mixer or stir until smooth.

Pour the batter over the brown sugar mixture in the skillet. Arrange the banana slices evenly over the top but not too close to the edges of the skillet.

Bake the cake for about 35 minutes, or until a toothpick inserted in the center comes out clean.

Remove the cake from the oven and let it cool in the skillet for 10 minutes. The skillet will still be hot. Cover a baking sheet with foil and invert it on top of the skillet. Wearing oven mitts, hold the edge of the sheet and the large handle of the skillet with one hand and use the other hand as a guide to keep the sheet and skillet together as you turn them over as a unit. Remove the skillet from the inverted cake, then use an offset spatula to slide the cake from the sheet to a large plate.

Let the cake cool, then serve with whipped cream or ice cream.

pistachio spice cake

Adding pudding to a cake mix not only contributes flavor to the cake; it ensures that it will be super-moist, too. In this case, the unique taste of pistachio pudding is combined with the subtle spices of cinnamon in the cake mix to produce a moist and exotic-tasting cake. Serve this treat with pistachio ice cream, and you'll hit a home run!

TIME: 1 hour

SERVES 8

2 tablespoons butter

2 tablespoons light brown sugar

1 box instant pistachio pudding mix

2 cups cold milk

1 box spice cake mix

½ cup vegetable oil

3 large eggs

½ cup roasted pistachios, shelled

Pistachio ice cream or whipped cream, for serving (optional)

Preheat the oven to 350°F.

Melt the butter in a 12- or 12½-inch cast iron skillet over low heat, then sprinkle the brown sugar evenly over the butter and keep warm on low heat while preparing the batter. Don't let the mixture burn. If your burner has a very low setting, that's best. If the mixture starts to get too brown, remove the skillet from the burner.

Combine the pudding mix and cold milk in a large bowl and whisk for 2 to 3 minutes, or until the pudding thickens. Add the cake mix, oil, and eggs and beat with an electric mixer or stir until smooth.

Pour the batter over the brown sugar mixture in the skillet. Scatter the pistachios evenly over the top but not too close to the edges of the skillet.

Bake the cake for about 35 minutes, or until a toothpick inserted in the center comes out clean.

Remove the cake from the oven and let it cool in the skillet for 10 minutes. The skillet will still be hot. Cover a baking sheet with foil and invert it on top of the skillet. Wearing oven mitts, hold the edge of the sheet and the large handle of the skillet with one hand and use the other hand as a guide to keep the sheet and skillet together as you turn them over as a unit. Remove the skillet from the inverted cake, then use an offset spatula to slide the cake from the sheet to a large plate.

Let the cake cool slightly, then serve with pistachio ice cream or whipped cream.

apple spice cake

Here's a fall classic that you'll want to make over and over again, especially when stores are loaded with a variety of your favorite freshly-picked apples. The nice thing about dump cakes is that they are just so darn easy to throw together—you can make them as often as you like.

TIME: 1 hour

SERVES 8

3 tablespoons butter

2 tablespoons dark brown sugar

½ teaspoon ground cinnamon

1 box spice cake mix

6 ounces unsweetened applesauce

3 large eggs

½ cup vegetable oil

1 large apple, cored, peeled, and cut into small pieces

1 to 2 tablespoons flour

⅓ cup apple butter

Whipped cream or ice cream, for serving (optional)

Preheat the oven to 350°F.

Melt the butter in a 12- or 12½-inch cast iron skillet over low heat, then sprinkle the brown sugar and cinnamon evenly over the butter. Keep warm over low heat, but if it starts to get too brown, remove the skillet from the burner.

Combine the cake mix, applesauce, eggs, and oil in a large bowl and beat with an electric mixer or stir until smooth. Put the apple pieces in a small bowl and dust them with just enough flour to coat. Fold the dusted apple pieces into the cake batter.

Pour the batter over the sugar mixture in the skillet and spoon the apple butter over the top.

Bake the cake for 35 to 40 minutes, or until a toothpick inserted in the center comes out clean.

Remove the cake from the oven and let it cool in the skillet for 10 minutes. The skillet will still be hot. Cover a baking sheet with foil and invert it on top of the skillet. Wearing oven mitts, hold the edge of the sheet and the large handle of the skillet with one hand and use the other hand as a guide to keep the sheet and skillet together as you turn them over as a unit. Remove the skillet from the inverted cake, then use an offset spatula to slide the cake from the sheet to a large plate.

Let the cake cool, then serve with whipped cream or ice cream.

Nutty Nutmeg Spice Cake

It occurred to me that I could enhance a spice cake mix by simply adding plenty of freshly-grated nutmeg and a generous amount of toasted walnuts to the batter. The added spice amps up the otherwise subtle nutmeg flavor, and the walnuts add real earthiness. If you make this cake in the fall, and you can find pumpkin ice cream in the stores, go for it. It's the perfect pairing, but French vanilla works, too.

TIME: 1 hour

SERVES 8

1½ cups walnut pieces, toasted and cooled

1 box spice cake mix

2 tablespoons butter

2 tablespoons light brown sugar

½ cup vegetable oil

6 ounces unsweetened applesauce

3 large eggs

½ cup water

1 teaspoon ground nutmeg

Pumpkin or French vanilla ice cream, for serving (optional)

Preheat the oven to 350°F.

Put the toasted walnuts in a small bowl and dust them with just enough of the cake mix to coat.

Melt the butter in a 12- or 12½-inch cast iron skillet over low heat, then sprinkle the brown sugar over the butter. Keep warm over low heat. If the mixture starts to get too brown, remove the skillet from the burner.

Combine the remaining cake mix, oil, applesauce, eggs, water, and nutmeg in a large bowl and beat with an electric mixer or stir until smooth. Fold the dusted walnuts into the batter.

Pour the batter over the sugar mixture in the skillet.

Bake the cake for 35 to 40 minutes, or until a toothpick inserted in the center comes out clean.

Remove the cake from the oven and let it cool in the skillet for 10 minutes. The skillet will still be hot. Cover a baking sheet with foil and invert it on top of the skillet. Wearing oven mitts, hold the edge of the sheet and the large handle of the skillet with one hand and use the other hand as a guide to keep the sheet and skillet together as you turn them over as a unit. Remove the skillet from the inverted cake, then use an offset spatula to slide the cake from the sheet to a large plate.

Let the cake cool, then serve with ice cream.

Port Wine Spice Cake

Port is wine that's been aged in oak barrels and then fortified with brandy. It's strong, sweet, and absolutely delicious! Here, the port is added to the butter in the skillet before the batter is poured in, so it contributes a boozy sweetness and a lovely (dark brown-purplish) tint to the crusty top of the inverted cake.

TIME: 1 hour

SERVES 8

3 tablespoons butter

½ cup port wine

1 box spice cake mix

6 ounces unsweetened applesauce

3 large eggs

½ cup vegetable oil

½ cup water

½ teaspoon almond extract

Whipped cream or ice cream, for serving (optional)

Preheat the oven to 350°F.

Melt the butter in a 12- or 12½-inch cast iron skillet over low heat, then add the port wine, stirring to combine. Keep warm over low heat while preparing the batter. If your burner has a very low setting, that's best. If the mixture starts to bubble, remove the skillet from the burner.

Combine the cake mix, applesauce, eggs, oil, water, and almond extract in a large bowl and beat with an electric mixer or stir until smooth.

Pour the batter over the port mixture in the skillet.

Bake the cake for 35 to 40 minutes, or until a toothpick inserted in the center comes out clean.

Remove the cake from the oven and let it cool in the skillet for 10 minutes. The skillet will still be hot. Cover a baking sheet with foil and invert it on top of the skillet. Wearing oven mitts, hold the edge of the sheet and the large handle of the skillet with one hand and use the other hand as a guide to keep the sheet and skillet together as you turn them over as a unit. Remove the skillet from the inverted cake, then use an offset spatula to slide the cake from the sheet to a large plate.

Let the cake cool, then serve with whipped cream or ice cream.

Lemony Spice Cake

Whenever you can add lots of lemon juice and lemon zest to a batter, as I have here, the cake is sure to come alive. But what I like most about this spice cake is the addition of lemon yogurt—it reinforces the brightness and flavor of the lemon and introduces a bit of tangy goodness. But don't worry, a drizzle of sugary lemon syrup to the top of the batter balances everything out.

TIME: 1 hour

SERVES 8

2 tablespoons butter

1 box spice cake mix

8 ounces lemon yogurt

3 large eggs

½ cup water

1 tablespoon lemon zest

½ cup fresh lemon juice

2 tablespoons confectioners' sugar

Whipped cream or ice cream, for serving (optional)

Preheat the oven to 350°F.

Melt the butter in a 12- or 12½-inch cast iron skillet over low heat while preparing the batter. Don't let the butter burn. If your burner has a very low setting, that's best. If the butter starts to brown, remove the skillet from the burner.

Combine the cake mix, yogurt, eggs, water, and lemon zest and beat with an electric mixer or stir until smooth. Combine the lemon juice and confectioners' sugar in a small bowl and stir until well combined.

Pour the batter over the butter in the skillet and drizzle the lemon glaze evenly over the top.

Bake the cake for 35 to 40 minutes, or until a toothpick inserted in the center comes out clean.

Remove the cake from the oven and let it cool in the skillet for 10 minutes. The skillet will still be hot. Cover a baking sheet with foil and invert it on top of the skillet. Wearing oven mitts, hold the edge of the sheet and the large handle of the skillet with one hand and use the other hand as a guide to keep the sheet and skillet together as you turn them over as a unit. Remove the skillet from the inverted cake, then use an offset spatula to slide the cake from the sheet to a large plate.

Let the cake cool, then serve with whipped cream or ice cream.

Spiced Rum Cake

There's something decadent about rum in a cake, particularly in a spice cake, but if you don't want to use the real thing here, you can substitute non-alcoholic rum extract instead. If you do use real rum, consider spiking the whipped cream, too. It makes a difference. You could flavor the whipped cream with the rum extract if desired, but I prefer not to.

TIME: 1 hour

SERVES 8

3 tablespoons butter

½ cup dark or spiced rum, or 1 tablespoon
non-alcoholic rum extract

2 tablespoons dark brown sugar

1 box spice cake mix

6 ounces unsweetened applesauce

3 large eggs

½ cup vegetable oil

½ cup water

Whipped cream or ice cream, for serving (optional)

Preheat the oven to 350°F.

Melt the butter in a 12- or 12½-inch cast iron skillet over low heat, then add the rum and stir gently until combined. Sprinkle the brown sugar evenly over the rum mixture and keep warm over low heat while preparing the batter. If your burner has a very low setting, that's best. If the mixture starts to bubble, remove the skillet from the burner.

Combine the cake mix, applesauce, eggs, oil, and water in a large bowl and beat with an electric mixer or stir until smooth.

Pour the batter over the rum mixture in the skillet.

Bake the cake for 35 to 40 minutes, or until a toothpick inserted in the center comes out clean.

Remove the cake from the oven and let it cool in the skillet for 10 minutes. The skillet will still be hot. Cover a baking sheet with foil and invert it on top of the skillet. Wearing oven mitts, hold the edge of the sheet and the large handle of the skillet with one hand and use the other hand as a guide to keep the sheet and skillet together as you turn them over as a unit. Remove the skillet from the inverted cake, then use an offset spatula to slide the cake from the sheet to a large plate.

Let the cake cool, then serve with whipped cream or ice cream.

Lemon Cakes

'D BE LOST WITHOUT LEMONS. I love their big, bold, tart taste! To me, lemons represent sunshine and sparkle, and my goal here was to offer a variety of lemon cakes that offer that "wow" lemony flavor and goodness. Because the purpose of these dump cakes is to keep things simple while maximizing flavor, a lemon cake mix serves as the foundation for each of these recipes, and I added fresh lemon juice (and sometimes lemon zest, too) to add even more lemon flavor and acidity and bump up all the other ingredients. Many of your favorite lemon flavor pairings—coconut, raspberries, cherries, nuts, poppy seeds—take a bow, but there are a few surprises here, too. Who knew that a Lemon Latte Cake, made with cold coffee, could steal the show? (It's the perfect afternoon treat!) And, as with all dump cakes, all you need is a dollop of whipped cream or a scoop of ice cream for a sweet finish. Several cakes just need a simple drizzle of melted jam or warm honey. Hungry yet?

Lemon-Cherry Cake

In our refrigerator, half-opened jars of jam can linger for, well, quite a while. We had one such jar of cherry jam, so I thought, "I'll melt it and add it to a lemon dump cake!" It worked like a charm. You can use almost any flavor of jam, from blackberry to apricot or grape. Have fun experimenting.

TIME: 1 hour

SERVES 8

2 tablespoons butter

1 box lemon cake mix

1 cup water

3 large eggs

⅓ cup vegetable oil

Juice from half a lemon

¼ cup cherry jam

Fresh whipped cream or any fruit-flavored ice cream, for serving (optional)

Preheat the oven to 350°F.

Melt the butter in a 12- or 12½-inch cast iron skillet over low heat while preparing the batter. Don't let the butter burn. If your burner has a very low setting, that's best. If the butter starts to brown, remove the skillet from the burner.

Combine the cake mix, water, eggs, oil, and lemon juice in a large bowl and beat with an electric mixer or stir until smooth.

Pour the batter over the butter in the skillet. Put the jam in a microwave-safe bowl and microwave on high for 10 seconds, or until melted. Stir until smooth. Swirl the melted jam over the top of the batter, then gently slice through with a knife to distribute it.

Bake the cake for 40 to 45 minutes, or until a toothpick inserted in the center comes out clean.

Remove the cake from the oven and let it cool in the skillet for 10 minutes. The skillet will still be hot. Cover a baking sheet with foil and invert it on top of the skillet. Wearing oven mitts, hold the edge of the sheet and the large handle of the skillet with one hand and use the other hand as a guide to keep the sheet and skillet together as you turn them over as a unit. Remove the skillet from the inverted cake, then use an offset spatula to slide the cake from the sheet to a large plate.

Let the cake cool, then serve with whipped cream or any fruit-flavored ice cream.

Lemon-Coconut Cake

The addition of fresh-squeezed lemon juice brings out the bright citrus in this cake, and the coconut sautéed in butter forms a nice topping when inverted. Look for coconut gelato or ice cream at your grocery store to serve with this lovely tropical treat.

TIME: 1 hour

SERVES 8

2 tablespoons butter

2 tablespoons light brown sugar

½ cup unsweetened coconut flakes

1 box lemon cake mix

1 cup coconut milk (or regular water)

3 large eggs

⅓ cup vegetable oil

Juice from half a lemon

Coconut gelato or coconut ice cream, for serving (optional)

Preheat the oven to 350°F.

Melt the butter in a 12- or 12½-inch cast iron skillet over low heat, then sprinkle with brown sugar and stir until melted. Sprinkle the coconut flakes over the sugar mixture and keep warm on low heat while preparing the batter. Don't let the coconut burn. If your burner has a very low setting, that's best. If the coconut starts to brown, remove the skillet from the burner.

Combine the cake mix, coconut milk, eggs, oil, and lemon juice in a large bowl and beat with an electric mixer or stir until smooth.

Pour the batter over the coconut in the skillet.

Bake the cake for 35 to 40 minutes, or until a toothpick inserted in the center comes out clean.

Remove the cake from the oven and let it cool in the skillet for 10 minutes. The skillet will still be hot. Cover a baking sheet with foil and invert it on top of the skillet. Wearing oven mitts, hold the edge of the sheet and the large handle of the skillet with one hand and use the other hand as a guide to keep the sheet and skillet together as you turn them over as a unit. Remove the skillet from the inverted cake, then use an offset spatula to slide the cake from the sheet to a large plate.

Let the cake cool, then serve with coconut gelato or ice cream.

Limoncello cake

Italians love their lemons, and their limoncello liqueur offers a concentrated lemon flavor. Add a splash of this to a lemon cake and the tart flavor comes alive, but with a bit of sweetness, too. A scoop of vanilla ice cream makes for an ideal finish.

TIME: 1 hour

SERVES 8

2 tablespoons butter

1 box lemon cake mix

¾ cup milk

¼ cup limoncello liqueur

3 large eggs

⅓ cup vegetable oil

Juice from half a lemon

Vanilla ice cream, for serving (optional)

Preheat the oven to 350°F.

Melt the butter in a 12- or 12½-inch cast iron skillet over low heat while preparing the batter. Don't let the butter burn. If your burner has a very low setting, that's best. If the butter starts to brown, remove the skillet from the burner.

Combine the cake mix, milk, limoncello, eggs, oil, and lemon juice in a large bowl and beat with an electric mixer or stir until smooth.

Pour the batter over the butter in the skillet.

Bake the cake for 35 to 40 minutes, or until a toothpick inserted in the center comes out clean.

Remove the cake from the oven and let it cool in the skillet for 10 minutes. The skillet will still be hot. Cover a baking sheet with foil and invert it on top of the skillet. Wearing oven mitts, hold the edge of the sheet and the large handle of the skillet with one hand and use the other hand as a guide to keep the sheet and skillet together as you turn them over as a unit. Remove the skillet from the inverted cake, then use an offset spatula to slide the cake from the sheet to a large plate.

Let the cake cool, then serve with vanilla ice cream.

Lemon-pecan cake

There's a certain sweetness in pecans that goes really well with the acidity of lemons. Here, a buttery salted pecan topping makes this lemony cake very special.

TIME: 1 hour

SERVES 8

½ cup salted pecan pieces

3 tablespoons butter

2 tablespoons dark brown sugar

1 box lemon cake mix

1 cup water

3 large eggs

6 ounces unsweetened applesauce

Juice from half a lemon

Whipped cream, for serving (optional)

Preheat the oven to 350°F.

Put the pecan pieces in a sealable plastic bag. Using a rolling pin, break the nuts into pea-size pieces (don't over-crush them). Set aside.

Melt the butter in a 12- or 12½-inch cast iron skillet over low heat, then sprinkle with the brown sugar and stir until melted. Add the pecan pieces and stir to coat. Keep warm over low heat while preparing the batter. Don't let the mixture burn. If your burner has a very low setting, that's best. If the mixture starts to brown, remove the skillet from the burner.

Combine the cake mix, water, eggs, applesauce, and lemon juice in a large bowl and beat with an electric mixer or stir until smooth.

Pour the batter over the nut mixture in the skillet.

Bake the cake for 35 to 40 minutes, or until a toothpick inserted in the center comes out clean.

Remove the cake from the oven and let it cool in the skillet for 10 minutes. The skillet will still be hot. Cover a baking sheet with foil and invert it on top of the skillet. Wearing oven mitts, hold the edge of the sheet and the large handle of the skillet with one hand and use the other hand as a guide to keep the sheet and skillet together as you turn them over as a unit. Remove the skillet from the inverted cake, then use an offset spatula to slide the cake from the sheet to a large plate.

Let the cake cool, then serve with fresh whipped cream.

Lemon Poppy Seed Cake

Here's another cake to keep in mind for an afternoon treat, or for breakfast, too. For me, it's the coffee connection; I just love having a coffee with something lemony. Just a thin slice of this cake with a dab of lemon curd always does the trick!

TIME: 1 hour

SERVES 8

2 tablespoons butter

1 box lemon cake mix

1 cup water

3 large eggs

6 ounces unsweetened applesauce

Juice from half a lemon

1 tablespoon poppy seeds

Lemon curd, grated lemon zest, and fresh mint, for serving (optional)

Preheat the oven to 350°F.

Melt the butter in a 12- or 12½-inch cast iron skillet over low heat while preparing the batter. Don't let the butter burn. If your burner has a very low setting, that's best. If the butter starts to brown, remove the skillet from the burner.

Combine the cake mix, water, eggs, applesauce, and lemon juice in a large bowl and beat with an electric mixer or stir until smooth.

Pour the batter over the butter in the skillet, then sprinkle the poppy seeds evenly over the top.

Bake the cake for 40 to 45 minutes, or until a toothpick inserted in the center comes out clean.

Remove the cake from the oven and let it cool in the skillet for 10 minutes. The skillet will still be hot. Cover a baking sheet with foil and invert it on top of the skillet. Wearing oven mitts, hold the edge of the sheet and the large handle of the skillet with one hand and use the other hand as a guide to keep the sheet and skillet together as you turn them over as a unit. Remove the skillet from the inverted cake, then use an offset spatula to slide the cake from the sheet to a large plate.

Let the cake cool, then serve with lemon curd, grated lemon zest, and fresh mint.

Variation: *Adding a fiber-rich cranberry topping to this cake complements the nuttiness of the poppy seeds and the tartness of the lemon. To add the cranberries to the butter mixture,* **increase the amount of butter to 3 tablespoons.** *Melt the butter in the cast iron skillet over low heat, then scatter* **½ cup whole fresh cranberries** *over the butter and cook over medium heat, stirring for 3 to 5 minutes, or until they begin to pop. Reduce the heat to very low heat and keep warm while you prepare the batter. Make sure that the berry mixture doesn't burn. If the burner gets too hot, remove the skillet from the heat. Continue to make the cake as directed.*

Lemon-Honey Cake

Bright-yellow lemons and deep golden honey—put them together, and you have a cake that shines with goodness. Don't forget to drizzle some honey on the cake while it's still warm.

TIME: 1 hour

SERVES 8

2 tablespoons butter

1 box lemon cake mix

1 cup milk

3 large eggs

6 ounces unsweetened applesauce

Juice from half a lemon

2 tablespoons honey, plus more for drizzling

Preheat the oven to 350°F.

Melt the butter in a 12- or 12½-inch cast iron skillet over low heat while preparing the batter. Don't let the butter burn. If your burner has a very low setting, that's best. If the butter starts to brown, remove the skillet from the burner.

Combine the cake mix, milk, eggs, applesauce, lemon juice, and 2 tablespoons honey in a large bowl and beat with an electric mixer or stir until smooth.

Pour the batter over the butter in the skillet.

Bake the cake for 35 to 40 minutes, or until a toothpick inserted in the center comes out clean.

Remove the cake from the oven and let it cool in the skillet for 10 minutes. The skillet will still be hot. Cover a baking sheet with foil and invert it on top of the skillet. Wearing oven mitts, hold the edge of the sheet and the large handle of the skillet with one hand and use the other hand as a guide to keep the sheet and skillet together as you turn them over as a unit. Remove the skillet from the inverted cake, then use an offset spatula to slide the cake from the sheet to a large plate.

While the cake is still warm, drizzle with additional honey.

Buttery Lemon Cake

For an especially rich-tasting lemon experience, this is the cake to make. I decided to pull out all the stops by using plenty of creamy and rich ingredients, like butter and eggs for ultimate flavor and buttermilk for moisture and tang. (By the way, commercially made buttermilk has very little to do with butter; it is made by adding a bacterial culture to pasteurized sweet whole milk). This is the ideal cake to serve with afternoon tea or coffee, but don't rule it out for dessert whenever you want a lemon high.

TIME: 1 hour

SERVES 8

2 tablespoons butter

1 box lemon cake mix

1 cup buttermilk

3 large eggs

6 tablespoons butter, melted

Juice from half a lemon

1 teaspoon lemon zest

Ice cream, for serving (optional)

Preheat the oven to 350°F.

Melt the butter in a 12- or 12½-inch cast iron skillet over low heat while preparing the batter. Don't let the butter burn. If your burner has a very low setting, that's best. If the butter starts to brown, remove the skillet from the burner.

Combine the cake mix, buttermilk, eggs, melted butter, lemon juice, and lemon zest in a large bowl and beat with an electric mixer or stir until smooth.

Pour the batter over the butter in the skillet.

Bake the cake for 35 to 40 minutes, or until a toothpick inserted in the center comes out clean.

Remove the cake from the oven and let it cool in the skillet for 10 minutes. The skillet will still be hot. Cover a baking sheet with foil and invert it on top of the skillet. Wearing oven mitts, hold the edge of the sheet and the large handle of the skillet with one hand and use the other hand as a guide to keep the sheet and skillet together as you turn them over as a unit. Remove the skillet from the inverted cake, then use an offset spatula to slide the cake from the sheet to a large plate.

Let the cake cool, then serve with ice cream.

Lemon Latte Cake

Coffee in a lemon cake—why not? I liked the idea of adding some earthiness to a lemon cake, and since I've been known to have a latte with almost anything, I decided to give this pairing a try. It's a winner in my book, and hopefully yours, too.

TIME: 1 hour

SERVES 8

2 tablespoons butter

1 box lemon cake mix

½ cup brewed coffee or espresso, cold

½ cup milk

3 large eggs

6 ounces unsweetened applesauce

½ teaspoon vanilla extract

Coffee ice cream, for serving (optional)

Preheat the oven to 350°F.

Melt the butter in a 12- or 12½-inch cast iron skillet over low heat while preparing the batter. Don't let the butter burn. If your burner has a very low setting, that's best. If the butter starts to brown, remove the skillet from the burner.

Combine the cake mix, coffee, milk, eggs, applesauce, and vanilla extract in a large bowl and beat with an electric mixer or stir until smooth.

Pour the batter over the butter in the skillet.

Bake the cake for 35 to 40 minutes, or until a toothpick inserted in the center comes out clean.

Remove the cake from the oven and let it cool in the skillet for 10 minutes. The skillet will still be hot. Cover a baking sheet with foil and invert it on top of the skillet. Wearing oven mitts, hold the edge of the sheet and the large handle of the skillet with one hand and use the other hand as a guide to keep the sheet and skillet together as you turn them over as a unit. Remove the skillet from the inverted cake, then use an offset spatula to slide the cake from the sheet to a large plate.

Let the cake cool, then serve with coffee ice cream.

peachy Lemon Cake

As several recipes in this book prove, it's wise to have a variety of canned fruits on hand that can be used to make a quick dump cake. Here, I've combined the bright flavors of two amazing fruits—peaches and lemons—that work in perfect harmony by melding sweet and tart.

TIME: 1 hour

SERVES 8

2 tablespoons butter

1 box lemon cake mix

4 large eggs

Juice from half a lemon

1 (15-ounce) can diced peaches, with juice

Peach ice cream, for serving (optional)

Preheat the oven to 350°F.

Melt the butter in a 12- or 12½-inch cast iron skillet over low heat while preparing the batter. Don't let the butter burn. If your burner has a very low setting, that's best. If the butter starts to brown, remove the skillet from the burner.

Combine the cake mix, eggs, lemon juice, and juice from the diced peaches in a large bowl and beat with an electric mixer or stir until smooth. Gently fold in the peach pieces.

Pour the batter over the butter in the skillet.

Bake the cake for 40 to 45 minutes, or until a toothpick inserted in the center comes out clean.

Remove the cake from the oven and let it cool in the skillet for 10 minutes. The skillet will still be hot. Cover a baking sheet with foil and invert it on top of the skillet. Wearing oven mitts, hold the edge of the sheet and the large handle of the skillet with one hand and use the other hand as a guide to keep the sheet and skillet together as you turn them over as a unit. Remove the skillet from the inverted cake, then use an offset spatula to slide the cake from the sheet to a large plate.

Let the cake cool, then serve with peach ice cream.

Lemon-Raspberry Cake

The flavor combination of raspberry and lemon is fresh and forward and, well, pretty fantastic! Raspberries perfectly temper the acidity of lemon. This cake is a looker, too—yellow lemony cake dotted with bright purple-red raspberries. Keep it in mind for a party.

TIME: 1 hour

SERVES 8

2 tablespoons butter

1 box lemon cake mix

1 cup water

3 large eggs

6 ounces unsweetened applesauce

2 tablespoons fresh lemon juice

1 teaspoon raspberry extract, or ¼ cup raspberry juice from thawed frozen raspberries

½ cup fresh or frozen raspberries

Fresh whipped cream and fresh raspberries, for serving (optional)

Preheat the oven to 350°F.

Melt the butter in a 12- or 12½-inch cast iron skillet over low heat while preparing the batter. Don't let the butter burn. If your burner has a very low setting, that's best. If the butter starts to brown, remove the skillet from the burner.

Combine the cake mix, water, eggs, applesauce, lemon juice, and raspberry extract in a large bowl and beat with an electric mixer or stir until smooth.

Pour the batter over the butter in the skillet. Scatter the raspberries evenly over the top, pressing them lightly into the batter.

Bake the cake for 35 to 40 minutes, or until a toothpick inserted in the center comes out clean.

Remove the cake from the oven and let it cool in the skillet for 10 minutes. The skillet will still be hot. Cover a baking sheet with foil and invert it on top of the skillet. Wearing oven mitts, hold the edge of the sheet and the large handle of the skillet with one hand and use the other hand as a guide to keep the sheet and skillet together as you turn them over as a unit. Remove the skillet from the inverted cake, then use an offset spatula to slide the cake from the sheet to a large plate.

Let the cake cool, then serve with fresh whipped cream and fresh raspberries.

strawberry Cakes

THERE'S NOTHING PRETTIER or happier than pink cake! Yes, you can find strawberry cake mix in the grocery store. And while there's plenty of strawberry flavor in the cake mix itself, you'll want to add fresh berries (or, if necessary, thawed frozen berries) to the batter or serve them with the cake. You can't have enough strawberries with strawberry cake. Also, although all dump cakes made in a cast iron skillet don't need frosting, there's something about strawberry cake that begs for some. I haven't suggested anything much beyond a dollop of whipped cream or a scoop of ice cream to accompany these cakes, but you just might want to have some whipped topping like Cool Whip® or a can of whipped cream on hand so you don't have to go to any trouble when it's time to eat. Frosting your strawberry cake with white, fluffy stuff (and adding more strawberries or sprinkles) is like putting bows in a little girl's hair before she goes to a party—it just feels right, and it looks great, too!

strawberry "pepper" cake

I'm beginning this chapter with the simplest of strawberry cake recipes—a box mix and a can of soda. Dr. Pepper® is the ideal choice because it has hints of cola and dark cherry, both of which complement the strawberry perfectly. Enjoy!

TIME: 45 minutes

SERVES 8

2 tablespoons butter

1 box strawberry cake mix

20 ounces Dr. Pepper® soda, or other cherry cola soda

Whipped cream or ice cream, for serving (optional)

Preheat the oven to 350°F.

Melt the butter in a 12- or 12½-inch cast iron skillet over low heat while preparing the batter. Don't let the butter burn. If your burner has a very low setting, that's best. If the butter starts to brown, remove the skillet from the burner.

Combine the cake mix and soda in a large bowl and beat with an electric mixer or stir until smooth.

Pour the batter over the butter in the skillet.

Bake the cake for about 35 minutes, or until a toothpick inserted in the center comes out clean.

Remove the cake from the oven and let it cool in the skillet for 10 minutes. The skillet will still be hot. Cover a baking sheet with foil and invert it on top of the skillet. Wearing oven mitts, hold the edge of the sheet and the large handle of the skillet with one hand and use the other hand as a guide to keep the sheet and skillet together as you turn them over as a unit. Remove the skillet from the inverted cake, then use an offset spatula to slide the cake from the sheet to a large plate.

Let the cake cool, then serve with whipped cream or ice cream.

Deluxe Strawberry Cake

*Box cake mixes typically call for water, oil, and eggs.
By replacing the water with whole milk or buttermilk
and the oil with lots of butter, you get a velvety, moist
cake that is especially rich and flavorful. Top this luxe
cake with fresh strawberries and whipped cream for the
ultimate experience.*

TIME: 1 hour

SERVES 8

2 tablespoons, plus ½ cup melted butter

1 box strawberry cake mix

1 cup whole milk or buttermilk

3 large eggs

1 tablespoon fresh lemon juice

Fresh strawberries and whipped cream, for serving
(optional)

Preheat the oven to 350°F.

Melt 2 tablespoons butter in a 12- or 12½-inch cast
iron skillet over low heat while preparing the batter.
Don't let the butter burn. If your burner has a very low
setting, that's best. If the butter starts to brown, remove
the skillet from the burner.

Combine the cake mix, milk, eggs, and lemon juice in a
large bowl and beat with an electric mixer or stir until
smooth. When the batter is lump-free, quickly stir in
the melted butter until incorporated.

Pour the batter over the butter in the skillet.

Bake the cake for about 35 minutes, or until a toothpick
inserted in the center comes out clean.

Remove the cake from the oven and let it cool in
the skillet for 10 minutes. The skillet will still be hot.
Cover a baking sheet with foil and invert it on top of
the skillet. Wearing oven mitts, hold the edge of the
sheet and the large handle of the skillet with one hand
and use the other hand as a guide to keep the sheet and
skillet together as you turn them over as a unit. Remove
the skillet from the inverted cake, then use an offset
spatula to slide the cake from the sheet to a large plate.

Let the cake cool, then serve with fresh strawberries
and whipped cream.

strawberry cream cake

Because of the addition of heavy cream as a replacement for water or even milk, this "cream" cake has a richness and yumminess that only this indulgent ingredient can provide. Fantastic!

TIME: 1 hour

SERVES 8

2 tablespoons butter

½ cup fresh strawberries, cut into small pieces

1 box strawberry cake mix

1 cup heavy cream

3 large eggs

½ cup vegetable oil

Whipped cream, for serving (optional)

Preheat the oven to 350°F.

Melt the butter in a 12- or 12½-inch cast iron skillet over low heat while preparing the batter. Don't let the butter burn. If your burner has a very low setting, that's best. If the butter starts to brown, remove the skillet from the burner.

Put the strawberry pieces in a small bowl and dust with just enough cake mix to coat. Set aside.

Combine the remaining cake mix, cream, eggs, and oil in a large bowl and beat with an electric mixer or stir until smooth. When the batter is lump-free, gently fold the strawberry pieces into the batter.

Pour the batter over the butter in the skillet.

Bake the cake for 35 to 40 minutes, or until a toothpick inserted in the center comes out clean.

Remove the cake from the oven and let it cool in the skillet for 10 minutes. The skillet will still be hot. Cover a baking sheet with foil and invert it on top of the skillet. Wearing oven mitts, hold the edge of the sheet and the large handle of the skillet with one hand and use the other hand as a guide to keep the sheet and skillet together as you turn them over as a unit. Remove the skillet from the inverted cake, then use an offset spatula to slide the cake from the sheet to a large plate.

Let the cake cool, then serve with whipped cream.

Strawberry and Black Pepper–Rum Cake

If you are scratching your head over this strawberry, black pepper, and rum combination, you've probably never sprinkled pepper over strawberries for a bit of spiciness or added rum to your baking for a bit of exotic heat. Go ahead, live dangerously. I promise you, it's a very nice surprise.

TIME: 1 hour

SERVES 8

2 tablespoons butter

½ cup fresh strawberries, cut into small pieces

1 box strawberry cake mix

1 cup water

3 large eggs

½ cup vegetable oil

1 tablespoon freshly ground black or white pepper

1 tablespoon rum

Strawberry ice cream, for serving (optional)

Preheat the oven to 350°F.

Melt the butter in a 12- or 12½-inch cast iron skillet over low heat while preparing the batter. Don't let the butter burn. If your burner has a very low setting, that's best. If the butter starts to brown, remove the skillet from the burner.

Put the strawberry pieces in a small bowl and dust with just enough cake mix to coat. Set aside.

Combine the remaining cake mix, water, eggs, and oil in a large bowl and beat with an electric mixer or stir until smooth. Gently stir in the black pepper and rum until incorporated, then gently fold the strawberry pieces into the batter.

Pour the batter over the butter in the skillet.

Bake the cake for 35 to 40 minutes, or until a toothpick inserted in the center comes out clean.

Remove the cake from the oven and let it cool in the skillet for 10 minutes. The skillet will still be hot. Cover a baking sheet with foil and invert it on top of the skillet. Wearing oven mitts, hold the edge of the sheet and the large handle of the skillet with one hand and use the other hand as a guide to keep the sheet and skillet together as you turn them over as a unit. Remove the skillet from the inverted cake, then use an offset spatula to slide the cake from the sheet to a large plate.

Let the cake cool, then serve with strawberry ice cream.

Variation: *Although strawberry jam is a natural for this strawberry cake, you may want to experiment with other flavors. Blackberry jam, raspberry jam, even grape jam would all be good here. And, of course, you could add fresh berries or grapes to match the melted jam topping.*

strawberry Jam cake

Everyone in my family loves jam, and a swirl of strawberry jam adds a bit of panache to this cake. It also adds bites of jammy flavor and texture. The additional jam topping is just more of a good thing!

TIME: 1 hour

SERVES 8

3 tablespoons butter

1 box strawberry cake mix

1 cup water

3 large eggs

6 ounces unsweetened applesauce

1 cup strawberry jam

Fresh strawberries, quartered, for serving (optional)

Preheat the oven to 350°F.

Melt the butter in a 12- or 12½-inch cast iron skillet over low heat while preparing the batter. If the butter starts to brown, remove the skillet from the burner.

Combine the cake mix, water, eggs, and applesauce in a large bowl and beat with an electric mixer or stir until smooth.

Pour the batter over the butter in the skillet. Melt the jam in a small pan over low heat, stirring until smooth, then remove from the heat. (Alternatively, put the jam in a microwave-safe bowl and microwave on high for 10 seconds, or until melted. Stir until smooth.) Drizzle ½ cup of the melted strawberry jam evenly over the top of the batter, but not too close to the edges of the skillet, and reserve the remainder for topping the finished cake.

Bake the cake for 35 to 40 minutes, or until a toothpick inserted in the center comes out clean.

Remove the cake from the oven and let it cool in the skillet for 10 minutes. The skillet will still be hot. Cover a baking sheet with foil and invert it on top of the skillet. Wearing oven mitts, hold the edge of the sheet and the large handle of the skillet with one hand and use the other hand as a guide to keep the sheet and skillet together as you turn them over as a unit. Remove the skillet from the inverted cake, then use an offset spatula to slide the cake from the sheet to a large plate.

Let the cake cool, then top with the reserved melted jam and quartered strawberries.

strawberry–white chocolate chip cake

Whenever you are looking for a cake that will please both adults and children, remember this one. It's pretty and delicious, which will appeal to the kids, and isn't overly sweet, which keeps almost all adults happy.

TIME: 1 hour

SERVES 8

2 tablespoons butter

2 tablespoons light brown sugar

¾ cup white chocolate chips

1 box strawberry cake mix

1 cup water

3 large eggs

½ cup vegetable oil

1 teaspoon vanilla extract

Ice cream, for serving (optional)

Preheat the oven to 350°F.

Melt the butter in a 12- or 12½-inch cast iron skillet over low heat, then sprinkle the brown sugar over the butter and keep warm on low heat while preparing the batter. If the mixture starts to get too brown, remove the skillet from the burner.

Put the white chocolate chips in a small bowl and dust with just enough cake mix to coat. Set aside.

Combine the remaining cake mix, water, eggs, oil, and vanilla extract in a large bowl and beat with an electric mixer or stir until smooth. Gently fold the white chocolate chips into the batter.

Pour the batter over the brown sugar mixture in the skillet.

Bake the cake for 35 to 40 minutes, or until a toothpick inserted in the center comes out clean.

Remove the cake from the oven and let it cool in the skillet for 10 minutes. The skillet will still be hot. Cover a baking sheet with foil and invert it on top of the skillet. Wearing oven mitts, hold the edge of the sheet and the large handle of the skillet with one hand and use the other hand as a guide to keep the sheet and skillet together as you turn them over as a unit. Remove the skillet from the inverted cake, then use an offset spatula to slide the cake from the sheet to a large plate.

Let the cake cool, then serve with ice cream.

Strawberry-Jelly Bean Cake

This is a colorful, fun cake to serve at Eastertime, when jelly beans are abundant. Just be sure to add the jelly beans to the batter just before putting the cake in the oven, so they'll float in the cake.

TIME: 1 hour

SERVES 8

2 tablespoons butter

2 tablespoons light brown sugar

1 box strawberry cake mix

1 cup water

3 large eggs

½ cup vegetable oil

1 cup jelly beans

Whipped cream, for serving (optional)

Preheat the oven to 350°F.

Melt the butter in a 12- or 12½-inch cast iron skillet over low heat, then sprinkle the brown sugar over the butter and keep warm on low heat while preparing the batter. Don't let the mixture burn. If your burner has a very low setting, that's best. If the mixture gets too brown, remove the skillet from the burner.

Combine the cake mix, water, eggs, and oil in a large bowl and beat with an electric mixer or stir until smooth.

Pour the batter over the brown sugar mixture in the skillet. Just before putting the cake in the oven, sprinkle the jelly beans evenly over the top of the batter.

Bake the cake for 35 to 40 minutes, or until a toothpick inserted in the center comes out clean.

Remove the cake from the oven and let it cool in the skillet for 10 minutes. The skillet will still be hot. Cover a baking sheet with foil and invert it on top of the skillet. Wearing oven mitts, hold the edge of the sheet and the large handle of the skillet with one hand and use the other hand as a guide to keep the sheet and skillet together as you turn them over as a unit. Remove the skillet from the inverted cake, then use an offset spatula to slide the cake from the sheet to a large plate.

Let the cake cool, then serve with whipped cream.

strawberry party cake

Everyone loves sprinkles, so it's no wonder that "funfetti" cake mixes are so popular. Inspired by these cakes, I experimented with adding sprinkles to various different box mixes and found the combination of sprinkle colors and pink cake to be especially pretty. Keep this beautiful cake in mind for all your festive parties.

TIME: 1 hour

SERVES 8

2 tablespoons butter

2 tablespoons light brown sugar

1 box strawberry cake mix

1 cup water

3 large eggs

6 ounces unsweetened applesauce

¼ cup colored sprinkles

Ice cream (multiple flavors), for serving (optional)

Preheat the oven to 350°F.

Melt the butter in a 12- or 12½-inch cast iron skillet over low heat, then sprinkle the brown sugar over the butter and keep warm on low heat while preparing the batter. Don't let the mixture burn. If your burner has a very low setting, that's best. If the mixture starts to get too brown, remove the skillet from the burner.

Combine the cake mix, water, eggs, and applesauce in a large bowl and beat with an electric mixer or stir until smooth. Gently fold the sprinkles into the batter (don't over-mix).

Pour the batter over the brown sugar mixture in the skillet.

Bake the cake for 35 to 40 minutes, or until a toothpick inserted in the center comes out clean.

Remove the cake from the oven and let it cool in the skillet for 10 minutes. The skillet will still be hot. Cover a baking sheet with foil and invert it on top of the skillet. Wearing oven mitts, hold the edge of the sheet and the large handle of the skillet with one hand and use the other hand as a guide to keep the sheet and skillet together as you turn them over as a unit. Remove the skillet from the inverted cake, then use an offset spatula to slide the cake from the sheet to a large plate.

Let the cake cool, then serve with ice cream. Have as much fun with the ice cream as you'd like! Scoops of multiple flavors make any party more festive.

Blush Wine Strawberry Cake

I have a friend who marinates strawberries in blush wine and then serves them over pound cake. The strawberries and blush wine pairing is delicious, especially when served with the moist cake. So, I thought, why not add the blush wine to a strawberry cake mix cake? Why not, indeed!

TIME: 1 hour

SERVES 8

2 tablespoons butter

2 tablespoons light brown sugar

1 box strawberry cake mix

1 cup blush wine

3 large eggs

6 ounces unsweetened applesauce

¼ cup red sprinkles (optional)

Whipped cream, for serving (optional)

Preheat the oven to 350°F.

Melt the butter in a 12- or 12½-inch cast iron skillet over low heat, then sprinkle the brown sugar over the butter and keep warm on low heat while preparing the batter. Don't let the mixture burn. If your burner has a very low setting, that's best. If the mixture gets too brown, remove the skillet from the burner.

Combine the cake mix, wine, eggs, and applesauce in a large bowl and beat with an electric mixer or stir until smooth.

Pour the batter over the brown sugar mixture in the skillet. Distribute the red sprinkles, if using, evenly over the top. Bake the cake for 35 to 40 minutes, or until a toothpick inserted in the center comes out clean.

Remove the cake from the oven and let it cool in the skillet for 10 minutes. The skillet will still be hot. Cover a baking sheet with foil and invert it on top of the skillet. Wearing oven mitts, hold the edge of the sheet and the large handle of the skillet with one hand and use the other hand as a guide to keep the sheet and skillet together as you turn them over as a unit. Remove the skillet from the inverted cake, then use an offset spatula to slide the cake from the sheet to a large plate.

Let the cake cool, then serve with whipped cream.

Strawberry Berry Cake

Make this pretty cake whenever you can find great-looking fresh strawberries and blueberries. Of course, summertime is ideal for finding the best berries, but you can make this any time of the year with a 12-ounce bag of frozen mixed berries. During the summer months, be sure to serve this cake with lots of fresh fruit, too.

TIME: 1 hour

SERVES 8

4 tablespoons butter

½ cup fresh strawberry pieces

½ cup fresh blueberries

1 box strawberry cake mix

1 cup water

3 large eggs

½ cup vegetable oil

1 teaspoon vanilla extract

Confectioners' sugar, for garnish (optional)

Fresh strawberries and blueberries, for serving (optional)

Preheat the oven to 350°F.

Melt the butter in a 12- or 12½-inch cast iron skillet over low heat while preparing the batter. If your burner is too hot and the butter starts to brown, remove the skillet from the burner.

Put the strawberries and blueberries (frozen may be used, see headnote) in a small bowl and dust with just enough cake mix to cover. Gently shake the berries until they are coated.

Combine the remaining cake mix, water, eggs, oil, and vanilla extract in a large bowl and beat with an electric mixer or stir until smooth. Gently fold the dusted fruit into the batter (don't over-mix).

Pour the batter over the butter in the skillet.

Bake the cake for 35 to 40 minutes, or until a toothpick inserted in the center comes out clean.

Remove the cake from the oven and let it cool in the skillet for 10 minutes. The skillet will still be hot. Cover a baking sheet with foil and invert it on top of the skillet. Wearing oven mitts, hold the edge of the sheet and the large handle of the skillet with one hand and use the other hand as a guide to keep the sheet and skillet together as you turn them over as a unit. Remove the skillet from the inverted cake, then use an offset spatula to slide the cake from the sheet to a large plate.

Let the cake cool, then sprinkle with confectioners' sugar and serve with fresh berries.

Index

Note: Photo pages are in italic.